USING
COMMON WORSHIP:
Times and Seasons
Lent to Embertide

USING
COMMON WORSHIP:
Times and Seasons
Lent to Embertide
A Practical Guide

David Kennedy
with Jeremy Haselock
Introduction by Roger Greenacre

Church House Publishing
Church House
Great Smith Street
London SW1P 3AZ

Tel: 020 7898 1451
Fax: 020 7898 1449

ISBN   978–0–7151–2127–6

Published 2008 by Church House Publishing

Typeset in   11pt Sabon and 11.5pt Gill Sans
by RefineCatch Ltd, Bungay, Suffolk

Printed by   Cromwell Press Ltd, Trowbridge, Wiltshire

Contents

Contents

Foreword

In this past generation there has been nothing less than a revolution in worship patterns in the Church of England. The treasury that is *The Book of Common Prayer* remains our wellspring, but *Common Worship* has helped us better appreciate the contrasts afforded by the seasons of the Church's year. This has allowed churches to engage flexibly with local needs within and beyond their congregations.

Times and Seasons offers a rich banquet. The two *Using Common Worship: Times and Seasons* volumes help those who plan and lead worship to provide a balanced yet imaginative diet from within this banquet. As the Liturgical Commission shifts its focus to the formation of God's people through worship, so this series of books offers a set of invaluable tools for the planning and leading of worship.

Both *Times and Seasons* and the *Using Common Worship* 'companions', then, allow for an effective and imaginative engagement with the tradition of the Church. That broad stream of tradition includes both the best of Anglican worship and spirituality together with a blending of ancient sources and contemporary patterns. These newly honed tools will give the Church the opportunity to offer a still better 'sacrifice of praise and thanksgiving' to God in Jesus Christ our Lord.

✠ *Stephen Wakefield*
Chairman of the Liturgical Commission

Acknowledgements

We are grateful to the following for permission to reproduce copyright material:

The Hymn Society/Hope Publishing For 'Help us O Lord to learn' by William Watkins Reid (page 140), copyright © 1952 renewed 1987 The Hymn Society/Hope Publishing Company. Administered by CopyCare, P O Box 77, Hailsham BN27 3EF, UK; music@copycare.com Used by permission.

Stainer & Bell for 'For the fruits of all creation' by Fred Pratt Green (page 146), copyright © Fred Pratt Green 1970, Stainer & Bell Ltd, London, England; www.stainer.co.uk

Wild Goose Resource Group for 'I will light a light in the name of the Maker' by John L. Bell (page 133) from *A Wee Worship Book* (Wild Goose Publications 1999), copyright © 1999 WGRG, Iona Community, Glasgow G2 3DH, Scotland.

Introduction
Roger Greenacre

Easter: The Christian Passover

> Before the festival of the Passover, Jesus, knowing that his hour
> had come to pass from this world to the Father, having loved those
> who were his in the world, loved them to the end.
>
> *John 13.1*, New Jerusalem Bible

The centrality of Passover

You may be expecting this Introduction to take the beginning of Lent
as its starting point; to get a clear overall vision of this season, however,
it is better to start in the heart and centre of the period from Lent to
Pentecost, with the final Passover that Jesus was to keep with his
disciples in Jerusalem. It is from that mid-point that we then need to
work backwards to Ash Wednesday and forwards to the Day of
Pentecost.

You may think too that Easter is just about the resurrection. But it is,
in fact, the celebration of what we might call the Christian Passover, in
which we recall Christ's suffering, his victory over death and its role in
God's purpose for his creation. Unfortunately, the English word *Easter*
doesn't make us think of Passover whereas, much more helpfully, the
French have *Pâques*, the Italians *Pasqua* and the Danes *Påske* – all
derived from the Greek word *Pascha* (Passover) – to describe the
festival. The seventeenth-century Roman Catholic translators tried in
vain to introduce the word *Pasch* into the English Language, but the
word *Passover*, invented by that brilliant translator William Tyndale in
the reign of Henry VIII, was by then already firmly established.

Up to the time of the Council of Nicaea (AD 325) and the
'Christianization' of the Roman Empire by the emperor Constantine,
the liturgical year of the Christian Church was extremely simple.
Practically its only features were a weekly and an annual *Pascha* or

Passover. The content of both was the same: the celebration of the paschal mystery, the mighty acts of God in Christ centred on the cross and resurrection. The weekly celebration was of course Sunday, the Day of the Lord, the first day of the week and also the 'eighth day' – the first day not only of a new week but also of the new creation. This understanding derives from the biblical vision of God creating the world in six days and resting on the seventh. On this 'eighth day', the first of the new creation, he inaugurated eternal life through the resurrection of Jesus Christ. The Sunday celebration was already observed in New Testament times.

The annual celebration was *Pascha*, an all-night vigil culminating in the Eucharist at dawn. This was clearly in existence in the second century, and almost certainly originated in the desire of the earliest Jewish Christian communities to transform and reinterpret their celebration of Passover.

Although the English language has only an obscure word of Anglo-Saxon origin, *Easter*, to describe the Christian Passover, we do have the adjective *paschal*. The Prayer Book Easter Preface refers to the paschal lamb and we speak of the paschal candle and, more importantly, of 'the paschal mystery'.

'The paschal mystery' is a phrase that has become familiar to Roman Catholics since the Second Vatican Council and the subsequent liturgical reforms; in the Church of England it was introduced into *The Alternative Service Book* of 1980 for the Renewal of Baptismal Vows at Easter and retained in *Common Worship: Times and Seasons*:

> As we celebrate the resurrection of our Lord Jesus Christ from the dead, we remember that through the paschal mystery we have died and been buried with him in baptism . . . In baptism, God calls us out of darkness into his marvellous light.
>
> *Times and Seasons*, pp. 341–2

At this point it may be helpful to remind ourselves of the specifically biblical understanding of the word 'mystery'. Mystery (in Greek *mysterion*) refers to something which was once hidden and is still inaccessible to purely human wisdom, but which has now been revealed and unveiled in Christ (cf. Ephesians 3.9; Colossians 1.26) and is communicated to believers in the 'mysteries' or sacraments of the

Church. The phrase 'the paschal mystery' designates that aspect of God's plan and purpose for his creation which finds its focus in the cross and resurrection. However, it must not be viewed in isolation. It must be understood as part of God's total plan and purpose. The ultimate mystery is the Person of Christ himself. Creation and redemption are inextricably linked. This is why the Creation narrative from Genesis 1 is the first of the Old Testament readings at the Easter Vigil. The same is true of incarnation and redemption; the one cannot be understood without the other. This is why the phrase from Psalm 2, 'You are my Son, this day have I begotten you', is applied both to Christmas (Hebrews 1.1-6) and Easter (Acts 13.33).

Understandings of the Jewish Passover

Before we begin to explore the understanding of the paschal mystery in the Christian tradition, it is illuminating to look at its roots in the Old Testament. Here we encounter two rather different interpretations. The Greek word *Pascha* translates the Hebrew word *Pesach*, which means a passage, a transit. But who is the subject of this passage? The earlier tradition takes it to be God himself who, according to the Book of Exodus, *passed through* the land of Egypt to destroy the Egyptians (Exodus 12.12). It goes on to record the order given to Moses: 'It is the passover sacrifice to the Lord, for he *passed over* the houses of the Israelites' (Exodus 12.27).

In a later tradition, originating in Hellenistic (Greek-speaking) Judaism, it is the Israelites themselves who are the subject of the Passover – they *passed over* the Red Sea. The first tradition is theocentric, emphasizing the saving action of God; the second is anthropocentric, emphasizing the human experience of liberation. A particular historical event of liberation is seen as a model, even as an allegory, for every passing over from darkness to light, from bondage to freedom, from time to eternity. Ultimately, of course, these two interpretations are not mutually exclusive; both find their place in the theology and liturgy of the Jewish celebration of Passover up to the present day.

Understandings of the Christian Passover

Among early Christians, similarly, there were different interpretations of *Pascha* (the Christian Passover). The problem was compounded by the mistaken belief of writers such as Bishop Melito of Sardis (died c.190), who derived *Pascha* from the Greek verb *paschein*, to suffer. The rival interpretations led to bitter divisions between the Christians of Asia Minor and other churches. The first group, including Melito, came to be called the Quartodecimans (from the Latin word for fourteenth), because they observed the all-night *Pascha* on the fourteenth day of the month Nisan (the day on which the Jews immolated the paschal lamb). The other churches (notably the church of Rome) always observed it on a Sunday. However, it was only the date that was under dispute; there does not appear to have been any controversy about the content of the celebration. For both sides the *Pascha* contained the whole sweep of the history of salvation, prefigured in the Exodus story, centred upon the cross and resurrection of Christ and recalled in eager anticipation of Christ's return and final triumph.

What may perhaps surprise us today is the predominant emphasis, both in Asia Minor and Rome, on the passion in this 'Easter' celebration. However, it is always on the passion as the victory of the cross, in which is included the resurrection – the seal and confirmation of that victory. We need to remember that there was still a long way to go before Holy Week and Good Friday made their appearance; the Night of Easter was then – as it still must be today – a unitive celebration of the whole mystery of salvation in which cross and resurrection are inseparably bound up together.

However, alongside this totally christocentric and historical emphasis another tradition grew up at the beginning of the third century, rooted in Alexandria. This had a striking parallel with the Hellenistic Jewish tradition of Passover, which was unsurprising as Alexandria was at the heart of the Hellenistic Jewish world. Writing in Alexandria, Origen, for example, clearly demonstrated that the accurate translation of *Pascha* was not suffering but passage. For the writers in this tradition the true 'passage' lies not so much in the past as in the present and the future: the life of the Church and of every Christian must be an exodus, a moral and spiritual pilgrimage which begins when we first come to faith and finds its terminus in eternity, a passage to that which does not pass.

It was that towering genius of Latin Christianity, St Augustine of Hippo (died 430), who resolved the tension, bringing together the two traditions. He found the key to the solution in the verse from the Fourth Gospel (John 13.1) quoted at the very beginning of this

Introduction: 'Before the festival of the *Passover*, Jesus, knowing that his hour had come to *pass from this world to the Father*, having loved those who were his in the world, loved them to the end.' The Christian Passover is therefore nothing other than the passage of Jesus from this world to the Father. This vision has two other advantages. First, it links together the cross and resurrection and glorification of Jesus in one single dynamic movement. Jesus is not going *to* his death, but *by way of his death* to the Father. Second, it unites the passage of Jesus, the Head of the Body, and that of ourselves, the members of his Body, in what is again a single dynamic movement. The threefold Passover of Israel, Jesus Christ and the Christian Church is one and indivisible.

St Augustine had himself been baptized by St Ambrose of Milan during the Night of Easter of the year 387; it is not difficult therefore to imagine how that profound personal experience shaped his own perception of the paschal mystery. This association of baptism with the Easter Vigil had already been clearly stated by Tertullian in North Africa and Hippolytus in Rome at the beginning of the third century. A powerful influence in the establishment of this association must have been the assertion of St Paul in his letter to the Romans (6.3, 4):

> Do you not know that all of us who have been baptized into Christ Jesus were baptized into his death? Therefore we have been buried with him by baptism into death, so that, just as Christ was raised from the dead by the glory of the Father, so we too might walk in newness of life.

This passage is part of the New Testament reading introduced into the Easter liturgy in both the post-Vatican II Roman Catholic rites and modern Anglican rites. What must be counted as one of the most brilliant and profoundly pastoral of all modern liturgical innovations had already been introduced into the Roman liturgy some years earlier, in 1951: the solemn renewal of baptismal promises, made whether there is a font in the church or not and whether there are candidates to be baptized or not.

If what *Times and Seasons* calls simply 'The Easter Liturgy' is the climax not only of the season from Ash Wednesday to Pentecost but of the whole Christian year, this has implications both for our worship and for our theological understanding of the role of the cross and of the resurrection in the mystery of our redemption by Jesus Christ, 'who was handed over to death for our trespasses and was raised for our justification' (Romans 4.25). The Vigil will never have the easy and immediate popular appeal of the Midnight Eucharist of Christmas, and there will be some churches where it will never be possible to celebrate it in its entirety. This guide will nevertheless indicate what can be done in such circumstances; it is vital that cross and resurrection (Good Friday and Easter) should never be celebrated in isolation from each other; the Paschal Mystery in its unity and integrity should be proclaimed throughout this time.

We move now from the Night of Easter, first backwards to the 40 days of Lent and then forwards to the 50 days of Easter and Pentecost. These two seasons are of great antiquity; the separate commemoration of the days of Holy Week and Ascension Day came much later.

Lent

There was a time when Lent was seen as a free-standing period of penitence and self-discipline modelled on the 40 days spent by Our Lord in the wilderness after his baptism. We have now come to a better understanding of its purpose as a direct preparation for the keeping of Easter. Nothing makes this clearer than the presidential introduction provided in the liturgy of Ash Wednesday:

> Brothers and sisters in Christ, since early days Christians have observed with great devotion the time of our Lord's passion and resurrection and prepared for this by a season of penitence and fasting.
>
> By carefully keeping these days, Christians take to heart the call to repentance and the assurance of forgiveness proclaimed in the gospel, and so grow in faith and in devotion to our Lord.
>
> I invite you, therefore, in the name of the Church, to the observance of a holy Lent, by self-examination and repentance; by prayer, fasting, and self-denial; and by reading and meditating on God's holy word.
>
> *Times and Seasons*, p. 223

An earlier version of this text (in *Lent, Holy Week, Easter*) pointed out that this season was at first of particular concern to two groups of people: those who were preparing for baptism at Easter, and those excluded by sin who were to be restored to the Church's eucharistic fellowship. Progressively, however, all Christian people had come to recognize that they were being summoned during Lent to a renewal of their baptismal covenant and a deepening of their penitence.

The ashes of Ash Wednesday remind us that we are both mortals in need of resurrection and sinners in need of forgiveness. The eager looking forward to Easter, implicit in this beginning, is spelled out in one of the Lenten prefaces:

> As we prepare to celebrate the Easter feast
> with joyful hearts and minds
> we bless you for your mercy
> and join with saints and angels
> for ever praising you . . .
>
> *Times and Seasons*, p. 218

Passiontide and Holy Week

Although the Fifth Sunday of Lent is no longer called Passion Sunday – the real Sunday of the passion is rather Palm Sunday – it does introduce a change of emphasis into the liturgy, focusing in a more concentrated way on the passion of the Lord through prayers, hymns and readings.

When we come to Holy Week itself, and more particularly to the rites of Palm Sunday, Maundy Thursday and Good Friday, we need to be aware of the powerful influence of the fourth-century church of Jerusalem and its creative exploitation of the incomparable teaching aids provided by the Holy Places. After the Constantinian revolution, these had become the focus of Christian pilgrimage from all over the Empire, especially during Holy Week and Easter. This development is brilliantly described in *Egeria's Travels*, the travel diary of a pilgrim nun from Western Europe who came to Jerusalem at the end of the fourth century. Inevitably a change of emphasis came into the liturgical celebrations, bringing to them a historical and rememorative character. To a considerable extent this altered the earlier character of the primitive *Pascha*. It had previously been a unitive and eschatological celebration – one event which recalled the suffering, death and resurrection of Christ, and the promise of his coming again. Now, the entry into Jerusalem was remembered on Palm Sunday, the Last Supper on Maundy Thursday, the passion on Good Friday and the resurrection on Easter Day (in Jerusalem, each in the Holy Place associated with the event concerned). However, we must not exaggerate the extent of this transformation; the Holy Week liturgy, dramatic as it was and still is, never became simply a re-enactment. At least in the liturgical texts, the theological vision of the unity of the paschal mystery was never lost. The mystery continued to be seen primarily in sacramental terms and not just in terms of a theatrical representation of the successive events leading up to Christ's resurrection. So, for example, the palm branches of Palm Sunday are not a make-believe reconstruction of a past event but a present day act of faith in Christ as our King and Messiah and an acknowledgement of his triumph.

Holy Week reaches its climax in what is known as the Paschal Triduum – the period of three days from Maundy Thursday evening to the evening of Easter Day, the three-day 'passing over' from suffering and death to resurrection. This period of *three* days is highly significant; the Bible is full of allusive references to 'three days' and 'the third day'. These three days need to be kept as a unity, with a proper emphasis on each stage (including space given to the reticence and silence of Holy Saturday), for they mark out the crucial steps of Christ's Passover journey to his Father and consequently of our own Passover journey with him.

The traditional abstinence from celebrating the Eucharist on Good Friday and Easter Eve underlines this unity. The ancient custom of giving Holy Communion on Good Friday from the elements consecrated on Maundy Thursday evening does so even more strongly, demonstrating the truth so clearly affirmed by the twentieth-century French theologian Louis Bouyer, in *The Paschal Mystery* (London, 1951, p. 161):

> the Cross of Christ is not defeat but victory, because that which gives it its true meaning is not the execution accomplished . . . on Friday but the offering Jesus made of himself at the Last Supper on Holy Thursday.

'Not defeat but victory' is the message which shines through the passion narrative of St John, which dominates the Good Friday liturgy.

To quote another twentieth-century theologian, this time the Swedish Lutheran bishop Gustaf Aulén, in his book *The Faith of the Christian Church* (Philadelphia, 1960, pp. 217–18),

> Good Friday appears in its right perspective only when it is seen in the light of Easter. If the note of triumph is not present in preaching on the passion, this preaching has lost its Christian character.

One of the anthems provided in the Good Friday proclamation of the cross makes an unequivocal affirmation of this unity:

> We glory in your cross, O Lord,
> and praise you for your mighty resurrection;
> for by virtue of your cross
> joy has come into our world.
>
> *Times and Seasons*, p. 315

Within the unity of the Paschal *Triduum* Good Friday is, as we have tried to show, inseparably linked with Maundy Thursday, but is equally linked with Holy Saturday and with Easter. This is particularly evident in that part of the Easter Liturgy which is called 'The Service of Light', both in symbolic action (e.g. the marking of the Paschal Candle with the five 'nails' of the Passion) and in word (e.g. in the language of the *Exsultet* or Easter Song of Praise):

> It is right and good that with hearts and minds and voices
> we should praise you, Father almighty, the unseen God,
> through your only Son, Jesus Christ our Lord,
> who has saved us by his death,
> paid for us the price of Adam's sin,
> and reconciled us once again to you.
>
> For this is the Passover feast,
> when Christ, the true Lamb of God, is slain,
> whose blood consecrates the homes of all the faithful.
>
> This is the night when you first saved our ancestors,
> Freeing Israel from her slavery
> and leading her safely through the sea.

> This is the night when Jesus Christ vanquished hell,
> broke the chains of death
> and rose triumphant from the grave.
>
> This is the night when all who believe in him are freed
>   from sin,
> restored to grace and holiness,
> and share the victory of Christ.
>
> This is the night that gave us back what we had lost;
> beyond our deepest dreams
> you made even our sin a happy fault.
>
> Most blessed of all nights!
> Evil and hatred are put to flight and sin is washed away,
> lost innocence regained, and mourning turned to joy.
>
> Night truly blessed, when hatred is cast out,
> peace and justice find a home, and heaven is joined to earth
> and all creation reconciled to you.
>
> *Times and Seasons*, p. 411

Eastertide and Pentecost

Before the Council of Nicaea (AD 325) the *Pascha* already had its season of preparation in Lent and its 50-day prolongation concluding on the Day of Pentecost. Ascension Day came much later (towards the end of the fourth century); originally the whole 50-day season was a unitive celebration of the resurrection and glorification of Jesus Christ and the descent of the Holy Spirit. This period was described either as the *Pascha* or more commonly as *Pentecost*, a word meaning 'fiftieth', which was used to describe not just the fiftieth day but the whole period of 50 days; so, for example, the Canon 20 of Nicaea forbids kneeling for prayer 'in the days of the Pentecost'.

Recent liturgical reform has tried to recover something of this unity by suppressing the Whitsun octave, in which the celebration of Pentecost continued for eight days, so that Pentecost now marks the definitive end of the Easter season and 'Ordinary Time' begins the next day. Instead, within the Easter season there is a nine-day period of expectant waiting from Ascension Day to Pentecost; in *Common Worship* this is characterized as 'days of prayer and preparation to celebrate the outpouring of the Spirit'. The character of the Feast of Pentecost as the consummation and completion of the Easter mystery is underlined. So in the Prayer after Communion we call upon God as the one 'who fulfilled the promises of Easter by sending us your Holy Spirit', while a concluding rite can include a gathering around the Paschal Candle before it is extinguished and removed from the sanctuary.

Easter and Pentecost belong to each other inseparably and indivisibly. We need perhaps to remember that in the Fourth Gospel (John 20.21-23) it is on the evening of the first Easter Day that Jesus breathes the Holy Spirit upon his disciples. So, paradoxically, we discover that Easter is a feast of the Spirit and Pentecost is a feast of Christ. The resurrection is itself an outpouring of the Holy Spirit by the Father upon the Son: Christ is raised by the Spirit, transformed by the Spirit, and in his resurrection has become 'a life-giving Spirit' (1 Corinthians 15.45). Conversely, at Pentecost we celebrate the new means of the risen Christ's presence with and to and for his people. We also celebrate the Church as the Body of Christ, but only and precisely because it is filled and vivified by his Spirit – remembering that the gospel records that the Spirit could not be given until Jesus was glorified (John 7.39).

Conclusion

It is recorded that when W. R. Inge, a twentieth-century Dean of St Paul's, was asked whether he was interested in liturgy, he replied, 'No; neither do I collect postage stamps!' This represents a tragic misunderstanding of the crucial role of the liturgy in the life of the Church. *Lex orandi* (the law of prayer) and *lex credendi* (the law of belief) must never be divorced. Their union is nowhere more vitally necessary than at this season of the Church's year, for the depth of meaning of the mystery of redemption is seriously weakened if it is not given its full liturgical and sacramental expression, and the liturgical rites themselves demand from all who participate in them a more profound awareness of their biblical and theological background.

1 More courses for the banquet

This is the second *Times and Seasons* volume in the *Using Common Worship* series. The first volume covered the period from All Saints' Day to Candlemas, and this volume embraces the rest of the *Times and Seasons* material, namely:

- Lent

- Passiontide and Holy Week

- The Easter Liturgy

- Easter

- Trinity to All Saints

- The Agricultural Year (including Embertide).

The first volume began with this quotation from Michael Marshall:

> [N]othing should be spared in trying to make certain that for *all* those who come to Church, nothing less than a banquet of word and worship is carefully prepared for each successive Sunday, or whenever and wherever God's people meet for worship.

The *Common Worship* project has indeed provided the Church of England with an unparalleled set of resources for worship. All the ingredients are there for a rich, nutritious and balanced diet. In some cases, a full menu has been provided, in the provision of fully worked-out services that can be reproduced in their entirety. In other places, there is the encouragement to do some creative experimenting, using combinations of material, adapted to local circumstances, from banks of resource material. At this point, it is worth setting out the full scope of the *Common Worship* provision:

- *Common Worship: Main Volume* (2000): essentially a 'Sunday Book', with all the principal services and a selection of resource material.

- *Common Worship: President's Edition* (2000): essentially for use at the holy table, but containing some material not available elsewhere.

- *Common Worship: Pastoral Services* (2nd edition, 2005): includes Wholeness and Healing, Marriage and Funeral liturgies.

- *Common Worship: Daily Prayer* (2005): an office book, includes Morning and Evening Prayer, Prayer during the Day, and Night Prayer, with supplementary resources.

- *Common Worship: Times and Seasons* (2006).

- *Common Worship: Christian Initiation* (2006): includes Baptism Confirmation, Rites on the Way, and Reconciliation rites.

- *Common Worship: Ordination Services* (2007).

- *Common Worship: Festivals* (2008): complementary to *Times and Seasons*, but for use at the holy table rather than as a 'directory' for use in service planning.

There are other associated resources, notably *New Patterns for Worship* (2002), a related but distinguishable resource book (see the Preface, pp. ix, x), as well as a series of *Common Worship* separates, including *Public Worship with Communion by Extension* (2001), *Series One Marriage and Burial Services* (2005) (both of which are now incorporated into the 2005 edition of *Pastoral Services*), and *Proclaiming the Passion: The Passion narratives in dramatized form* (2007).

While the focus here is on *Times and Seasons*, nevertheless part of planning and preparing the banquet is being aware of the other *Common Worship* publications, and how aspects of them can also be incorporated into the menu. This in itself is a major formational task, and it is hoped that this book is a contribution towards such cross-referencing.

Times and Seasons itself owes much to its predecessors: *Lent, Holy Week, Easter: Services and Prayers* (1986), *The Promise of His Glory* (1991) and *Enriching the Christian Year* (1993). It is also beginning to be adorned by supplementary publications, notably *Together for a Season*, a three-volume all-age resource book based around *Times and*

Seasons services. So far, two volumes have appeared covering Advent to Candlemas and Ash Wednesday to Pentecost. In time, further resources will appear, including musical settings.

The first volume of *Using Common Worship: Times and Seasons* set out the scope of the *Times and Seasons* material (pp. 14–18) and John Sweet's excellent Introduction teased out the understanding of 'liturgical time' that is fundamental to the creative use of this material (see pp. 10–12). His Introduction to the All Saints to Candlemas period is here complemented by Roger Greenacre's fine account of the Paschal cycle.

The aim of both volumes is to provide information to enable a proper understanding of the seasonal rites, as well as ideas of how they might be presented and executed. As with all publications bearing the *Praxis* name, the intention is to be inclusive of aspects of churchmanship, and so examples are given from broadly 'catholic', 'evangelical' and 'charismatic' traditions, as well as those who simply rejoice in the name 'Anglican' and wish to embrace insights from many traditions in the Church Catholic. So in good Delia, Jamie or Nigella fashion, happy cooking, for God's people deserve the best, *carefully* prepared and drawing on all that *Common Worship* can offer.

2 Lent
Jeremy Haselock

> When a man leaves on a journey, he must know where he is going
> . . . Above all, Lent is a spiritual journey and its destination is
> Easter, the Feast of Feasts.
>
> *Alexander Schemann*

The Lenten journey

As with all foreseen journeys, the Lenten journey requires careful
advance planning, a clearly defined route and a well-considered set of
resources – luggage that is helpful and not burdensome. This particular
journey is a pilgrimage and its goal is clear: the right celebration of
Easter. But Easter itself is not just a day; it is fifty days of celebration, a
week of weeks, and so the journey can truly be said to be 'from ashes
to fire', from the penitential cinders of Ash Wednesday to the
inspirational flames of Pentecost.

At the core of *Common Worship: Times and Seasons*, from pages 210
to 502, there are the resources for the liturgical celebration of this period
of the Christian year. They celebrate those saving acts of God in Christ
which stand at the very heart of our faith. This segment of the liturgical
year, embracing Lent, Holy Week and Eastertide, needs to be seen as a
unity (admittedly containing within itself smaller unities), approached
holistically, and consequently planned carefully and thoroughly from
beginning to end.

In this chapter we consider the first four weeks of the season of Lent,
from Ash Wednesday until the Saturday after the Fourth Sunday in Lent.
Passiontide and Holy Week will be dealt with in the next chapter. The
Times and Seasons provision is:

- Introduction to the Season
- Seasonal Material

- The Liturgy of Ash Wednesday

- The Way of the Cross.

The lectionary

As our journey progresses, the real significance of Lent is gradually revealed through the readings appointed for the principal service on Sundays and the weekday eucharistic lectionary for the season. A quick but representative overview reveals three distinct but related themes: Penitence and self-denial; Christian baptism; and the Lord's passion.

The readings from Ash Wednesday until the end of the second week of Lent illustrate the first theme with such passages as the repentance of Nineveh at the preaching of Jonah (Jonah 3.1-10), Daniel's confession of the sins of Israel (Daniel 9.4-10), the parable of the sheep and goats (Matthew 25.31-46), Christ's call for us to be reconciled to our brother (Matthew 5.20-26), and the parable of the prodigal son (Luke 15.11-32).

From the third Sunday the baptismal theme begins to emerge more strongly with the healing of Naaman in the waters of the Jordan (2 Kings 5.1-15), the stream of water issuing from the Temple (Ezekiel 47), and the three classic passages from John's Gospel used from the earliest times for the instruction of candidates for baptism: the Samaritan woman at the well (John 4), the healing of the man born blind (John 9), and the raising of Lazarus (John 11).

From the fifth Sunday the theme of the Lord's passion predominates with such readings as Moses and the brazen serpent (Numbers 21), and gospel passages from John chapters 8, 10 and 11.

The fact that these three themes are linked by their common relationship with Easter helps us, as we plan our liturgy, to understand that Lent does not exist for its own sake. It is nothing if it is not a preparation for Easter. Not only is it proximate preparation for baptism for those who have been following the enquirer's path towards faith; it is also a sort of corporate retreat for the whole congregation, enabling them to gain the maximum spiritual benefit from the liturgical celebration of Easter. Study groups, individual and corporate penitence, almsgiving and self-denial – all the traditional Lenten activities – are best planned within this liturgical framework. This is where they make the most sense.

Lenten austerity

Each seasonal section in *Times and Seasons* is prefaced by an Introduction to the Season which encapsulates as briefly as possible some of the distinctive qualities and 'liturgical flavours' of each time of the year. As the introduction to Lent points out, the season is characterized by self-examination, penitence, self-denial and almsgiving, study and preparation for the celebration of the paschal mystery. As far as self-denial is concerned, Canon B 6. 3 tells us that

> the days of Fasting or Abstinence and the Vigils which are to be observed in the Church of England are set out in *The Book of Common Prayer*, whereof the 40 days of Lent, particularly Ash Wednesday, and the Monday to Saturday before Easter, ought specially to be observed.

This personal austerity of life commended by the Canons is traditionally reflected in the liturgy of the Church and in the way in which the church building is decorated. The music of the liturgy might be more simple in Lent, with the organ or other musical instruments used only to sustain the singing. The Gloria in Excelsis is not sung at the Holy Communion service nor should the acclamation 'alleluia' be heard. Liturgical dress should be the simplest possible. Vestments, if worn, and altar frontals should be violet in colour or of unbleached linen of the type known as Lenten Array, and the church building is usually kept bare of flowers and other decorations. The Fourth Sunday of Lent, now usually observed as Mothering Sunday, used to be known as *Laetare* or Refreshment Sunday. Rose-coloured vestments may be worn as a mark of the respite from Lenten rigour permitted on this day.

Baptism

Since the earliest times Easter has been the privileged and chosen occasion for the celebration of the rites of Christian initiation. The observance of Lent, as we have seen, grew out of the desire of the Christian congregation to share at least some aspects of their preparation with those who were to be baptized. The recovery of this insight undoubtedly revitalizes Lent. If you plan to prepare candidates for baptism at Easter it is worth looking at how the traditional forms of service might be integrated with the material in 'Rites on the Way'. *Common Worship: Christian Initiation* proposes a number of seasonal patterns; the classical paschal pattern is pre-eminent and shown as

Pattern 1 (see table below). Anyone who has been present when baptism has been administered at the Easter Vigil, or indeed on Easter Day, will require little convincing that all the traditional paschal rites and ceremonies become clear, transparent and far more comprehensible when this essential component is restored. For this reason it is worth considering a baptismal approach to the whole season. This will be of as much help to the regular congregation of the baptized as it will be to those approaching the sacraments of Christian initiation.

Pattern 1 is explained comprehensively in the 'Commentary by the Liturgical Commission', appended to *Common Worship: Christian Initiation* (pp. 330–1), but it is worth summarizing here in tabular form, because it is so helpful in planning our celebration.

Pattern 1	**Initiation at Easter**
Call	The First Sunday of Lent
Presentation of the Four Texts	The Second, Third, Fourth and Fifth Sundays of Lent
Baptism, Confirmation (if bishop presides) Affirmation, Reception	Easter Vigil or Easter Day
Thanksgiving and Sending Out	Pentecost

The process of exploration leading to the beginning of the formal journey of faith will inevitably be long, whether undertaken privately or within a structured scheme of instruction such as Alpha or Emmaus. With this in mind, the preliminary liturgical rite, 'Welcome of Disciples on the Way of Faith', will have to be programmed several months before the beginning of Lent. An appropriate time for this Welcome might be at the end of September, around Michaelmas, when life begins again after the summer break. The Call then takes place as part of the principal service on the First Sunday of Lent, when the whole community is focusing on penitence, study and self-denial.

Following this scheme, the Four Texts are presented liturgically on the following four Sundays of Lent, with each of these key elements in the Christian knapsack being the focus of group study in the week after the presentation. Other resources are available in *Common Worship: Christian Initiation* to inspire short acts of worship within these group meetings. Likewise, items from the *Times and Seasons* Lent seasonal material section (pp. 212–20) may be included. On the Sundays the prayers of intercession should regularly make mention of those preparing for initiation. One of the fully worked-out prayers, H1 on page 215, shows how this may be done:

Baptism follows naturally at the Easter Vigil or on Easter Day, together with confirmation if the bishop is presiding. Those who are already baptized but are reaffirming their faith do so in the same context. Whether the bishop is there or not, it is appropriate that those who are baptized at Easter should be admitted to communion. Confirmation might then follow during the fifty days of Eastertide or at Pentecost. The Rites of Thanksgiving for Holy Baptism, the Commission and the Sending Out form a fitting conclusion to the staged initiation process as part of the Pentecost celebrations.

How should these liturgical staging posts on the journey of faith be integrated into the Sunday liturgy? In the Eucharist or a Service of the Word they would seem to fit in well and appropriately after the Sermon. However, you could also make the presentation of the Four Texts a part of the Dismissal at the end of the service. At the Eucharist the catechumens could be called forward from the congregation after the Prayer after Communion and the Texts presented before the blessing and dismissal. When the Apostles' Creed is delivered on the Third Sunday of Lent, any other Creed or Affirmation of Faith should probably be omitted from the service.

Excellent though this 'Rites on the Way' resource is, there is a danger in using too much of it in the usual Sunday liturgy and overloading the service with words. If a substantial proportion of the Four Texts supporting material is included, it would be worth thinking about which parts of the liturgy could be cut to restore a more even balance. One helpful solution might be to follow the structure of 'A Service of the Word with Holy Communion' on these occasions. Details of how to do this may be found in the *Main Volume* (pp. 25ff) and in *New Patterns for Worship* (pp. 21ff).

Seasonal material

Invitations to Confession Three forms are provided. The first, based on Psalm 51.17, appears in the Seasonal Provisions in the *Main Volume* for the period 'from Ash Wednesday until the Saturday after the Fourth Sunday of Lent'. The second is by David Silk, from his *In Penitence and Faith*, and is based on Daniel 9.9. The third is new to this compilation and is based on Luke 4.1,2, Christ's temptation by the devil, so is most suitable for the First Sunday of Lent, particularly in year C.

Kyrie Confessions Three forms are given. The first two are based on verses from Psalm 51 and come from the *Main Volume* and *New Patterns* respectively. The third is also from *New Patterns* and is a help to self-examination.

Gospel Acclamations It is important to remember that the acclamation 'alleluia' is by ancient tradition not uttered in Lent so that it rings out all the more gloriously at Easter. The Lenten forms offered here use the refrain, 'Praise to you, O Christ, King of eternal glory.' Of the four acclamations provided, the first is from the *Main Volume* Seasonal Provisions and is based on verses from Psalm 95. The others are drawn from James 1.12, John 8.12 and Psalm 119.105 respectively.

Intercessions Two full forms of intercession are provided, both taken directly from *Enriching the Christian Year*. The first form has a petition for those to be baptized (and confirmed) at Easter. As with all the fully worked-out forms of intercession provided in *Times and Seasons*, they can be used as they stand or as models for prayers more directly applicable to the pastoral situation of the praying community.

Introduction to the Peace The one form offered here is that given in the *Main Volume* and is based on Romans 5.1,2.

Prayers at the Preparation of the Table Two of the three prayers provided are adapted from Prayers over the Gifts in the Canadian *Book of Alternative Services*. The third is a new composition with resonance for those who are 'on the Way' and approaching baptism.

Two further prayers are provided in the fully worked-out Liturgy of Ash Wednesday. While these are particularly appropriate to the beginning of Lent, either may be used on any of the Sundays or weekdays of the season.

Prefaces Three short prefaces are provided. The first was originally drafted for Series 3, then included in the *ASB*, and is now in the *Main Volume*, for which it had a further clause added introducing the concept of preparation for the right celebration of the paschal mystery. The other two are reworkings of texts from the Canadian *Book of Alternative Services* and the *Roman Missal* respectively and brought into this collection from *Enriching the Christian Year*.

Extended Preface This also comes from the seasonal provision in the *Main Volume* and is a rich compilation identifying many of the significant themes to be found in the scriptural readings of the Lenten season. Incidentally, some people find it helpful to read the Extended Preface provided for the day or the season as part of their sermon preparation. Many of the phrases used can trigger a useful train of thought; this preface, for example, has many such rich phrases, including 'desert of repentance'; 'pilgrimage of prayer and discipline'; 'you bring us back to your generous heart'.

Blessings Two standard forms of blessing are given, from the *Main Volume* and the *ASB* respectively, and a solemn blessing from the *President's Edition*. These threefold solemn blessings should perhaps be used sparingly. They provide a more weighty conclusion to a service for landmark days and remind us at the end of a celebration of some of its major themes. As we shall see, this form is used at the end of the Liturgy of Ash Wednesday, but unless the bishop is presiding, for example, it is best not used on the following Sundays of Lent.

Acclamations Two are provided: the first a version of 1 John 4.10-12, the second from *Common Worship: Daily Prayer* where this form of acclamation is used daily at Morning and Evening Prayer.

It is perhaps worth a reminder of what *Enriching the Christian Year* had to say about how these acclamations can be used (p. xiv):

> Sometimes they might give a seasonal flavour to the service at the very beginning before the opening hymn or after the Greeting. They might also be used before, between or after readings. At a [Service of the Word] they could well be part of a climax at the end. A repeated two-line acclamation can be used repeatedly through a service, both to call people back to a theme, and also to mark the transition from one stage of the service to the next.

Short Passages of Scripture Five are provided here. The first two are useful opening sentences, the third might preface the Peace, and the final one could appropriately conclude a service as part of the blessing or dismissal.

Other resources

There are useful additional resources for Lent in *New Patterns*. The Resource Section has Lenten material under the headings 'Cross' and 'Lament'. There is an excellent model Service of the Word, entitled 'In Penitence and Faith: A Service for Lent' (pp. 396–401). Taking up the lament theme, another model service, 'Facing Pain: A Service of Lament' (pp. 443–8) could easily be adapted as a Lenten service, not least because the idea of lamenting over our sins, individual and corporate, is a primary Lenten theme. Similarly, 'A Penitential Service (outline)' (pp. 449–50) provides a basic structure which can then be clothed with material from the Resource Section.

Lent, Holy Week, Easter: Services and Prayers included two Services of Penitence, either of which could be used as a free-standing non-sacramental service or combined with a celebration of the Holy Communion (see Order A, pp. 39–46, and Order B, pp. 47–55).

Some of the *Lent, Holy Week, Easter* penitential material is adapted in 'A Corporate Service of Penitence' in *Common Worship: Christian Initiation* (pp. 228–63). Note 1 (p. 228) suggests that this service is suitable for use in Lent or any occasion 'when Christian communities wish to respond to the call of the gospel to a deeper repentance'.

A Corporate Service of Penitence has the following structure:

The Gathering
The Greeting
[Introduction]
The Comfortable Words
The Collect

The Liturgy of the Word
Readings and Psalm
Gospel Reading
Sermon

Prayer and Penitence
Prayers of Penitence
The Lord's Prayer – *unless Holy Communion is celebrated*

[The Liturgy of the Sacrament
The Peace
Preparation of the Table
Taking of the Bread and Wine
The Eucharistic Prayer
The Lord's Prayer
Breaking of the Bread
Giving of Communion
Prayer after Communion]

The Sending Out
Thanksgiving for Holy Baptism or Proclamation of the Gospel
The Peace – *unless Holy Communion is celebrated*
[Blessing – *if Holy Communion is celebrated*]
The Dismissal

The Prayer and Penitence section, as well as including a general confession, may also include

- the Beatitudes or an extended Form of Penitence based on the Beatitudes (see pp. 241–3)

- the Ten Commandments (two forms are given on pp. 244–5, the latter including the Old Testament commandment with a complementary New Testament reference; this can be read effectively by two voices)

- the Summary of the Law

- a Litany of Penitence (see p. 247)

- a Biblical Reflection on Penitence (see pp. 248–51)

- *Veni, Creator Spiritus*

- a penitential hymn or song

- or other forms of penitential material devised locally.

A Litany of Penitence is adapted from the Roman Catholic Rites of Penance:

Christ our Saviour is our advocate with the Father:
with humble hearts let us ask him to forgive us our sins
and cleanse us from every stain.

You were sent with good news for the poor
and healing for the contrite.
Lord, be merciful to me, a sinner.

You came to call sinners, not the righteous.
Lord, be merciful to me, a sinner.

You forgave the many sins of the woman who showed you
   great love.
Lord, be merciful to me, a sinner.

You did not shun the company of outcasts and sinners.
Lord, be merciful to me, a sinner.

You carried back to the fold the sheep that had strayed.
Lord, be merciful to me, a sinner.

You did not condemn the woman taken in adultery,
but said, 'Go and sin no more.'
Lord, be merciful to me, a sinner.

You called Zacchaeus to repentance and a new life.
Lord, be merciful to me, a sinner.

You promised Paradise to the repentant thief.
Lord, be merciful to me, a sinner.

You are always interceding for us
at the right hand of the Father.
Lord, be merciful to me, a sinner.

A Biblical Reflection on Penitence is drawn from the same source; the following extract gives a flavour of its scope:

We were reconciled to God by your death, Lord Jesus,
and will be saved by your risen life.
Lord, have mercy.

You died and were raised and sit at the right hand of God,
to make intercession for us.
Lord, have mercy.

You became for us wisdom from God,
and our righteousness, sanctification and redemption.
Lord, have mercy.

You washed us, you sanctified us, you justified us,
in your name and in the Spirit of our God.
Lord, have mercy.

When we sin against members of your family,
we sin against you.
Lord, have mercy.

Though you were rich, yet for our sakes you became poor,
so that by your poverty we might become rich.
Lord, have mercy.

You gave yourself for our sins
to set us free from the present evil age.
Lord, have mercy.

You rose from the dead to rescue us from the wrath that is
  coming.
Lord, have mercy.

The service concludes with either 'Thanksgiving for Holy Baptism' or 'Proclamation of the Gospel', a dismissal gospel reading that encourages the congregation to live in the light of forgiveness. Where the former is used, it underlines the insight that forgiveness recalls us to our baptismal status where sin has been dealt with and so we are called to walk in newness of life. This further emphasizes the baptismal themes that we have already considered above, and its use in Lent points us forward to the celebration of initiation and the corporate renewal of baptismal vows at Easter.

The resources section for A Corporate Service of Penitence also includes

- Invitations to Confession (p. 254)

- Kyrie Confessions (pp. 254–5)

- Lectionary material, including the following Lenten provision:

Old Testament	Exodus 20.1-17	Isaiah 53.3-6	Jeremiah 17.5-10, 14
Psalm	Psalm 51.6-12	Psalm 103.1-5, 8-14	Psalm 23
New Testament	1 John 3.4-10	Romans 5.6-11	2 Cor. 12.7b-10
Gospel	Luke 18.9-14	Mark 2.1-12	Mark 14.32-38
Dismissal Gospel	Luke 15.3-7	Mark 5.18-20	Mark 13.34-36

- Gospel Acclamations (the acclamations beginning 'Praise to you, O Christ . . .' are designed for use in Lent, p. 257)

- A Form of Intercession adapted from the *Book of Common Order* of the Church of Scotland (pp. 258–9)

- Introductions to the Peace (p. 261)

- Prayer at the Preparation of the Table, adapted from the Church of South India:

> Gather up, O Lord, the broken fragments of our humanity,
> that in your wounded hands we might find our healing.
> **Blessed be God for ever.**

- Prefaces (two short and one extended, adapted from the Roman Catholic Masses for Reconciliation, p. 262)

- Acclamation, drawing on the 'water of life' imagery of Revelation 21 (p. 263)

- Blessings and Ending (p. 263).

So, particularly for the season of Lent, this material provides significant additional resources, parts of which, of course, could be incorporated into regular eucharistic or non-eucharistic worship.

Ash Wednesday

Ash Wednesday is a Principal Feast in the *Common Worship* Calendar and is one of those holy days when, under Canons B 13 and 14, the Holy Communion must be celebrated in all places of public worship. *Times and Seasons* offers a fully worked-out Liturgy of Ash Wednesday for those who wish to honour this obligation. This service

exhibits the normative, fourfold structure of Order 1 Holy
Communion with a fifth element, a Liturgy of Penitence, between the
Liturgy of the Word and the Liturgy of the Sacrament. This basic
structure is enriched with seasonal material appropriate to the
beginning of Lent.

The Gathering

As would seem natural, the Ash Wednesday rite is heavily penitential
and this emphasis is explained in a presidential Introduction which
follows the Greeting. Roger Greenacre's introduction to this volume
has already mentioned this text, which locates what we are doing
historically in the tradition, briefly explains the purpose and
significance of Lent, and invites the assembly to observe a holy season
of preparation.

It helps the congregation to absorb this information prayerfully if the
Trisagion or some other suitable penitential hymn or song is sung
before the Collect. The text of the *Trisagion* is printed in this place in
the worked-out version. The *Trisagion* was originally a much used text
in the Orthodox and Oriental liturgies – indeed it is a hymn which
forms part of the fixed prayers at the beginning of all these services. It
is now often used in the West in a wide variety of contexts, but as we
shall see, its most familiar use is in the Reproaches in the Liturgy of
Good Friday.

Notice that the general confession and absolution, which would
normally appear at this point in Order 1, are omitted in favour of the
more extended Liturgy of Penitence later on in the service.

Two Collects are printed, the Collect for Ash Wednesday from the
Main Volume, which is a lightly modernized version of that in the *BCP*,
and the more economical contemporary collect from the additional
series authorized by General Synod in 2004, which is a new
composition.

The Liturgy of the Word

This follows standard format and the Principal Service readings from
the Lectionary should be used. These are the same for all three years of
the cycle but there are alternative First Readings and Gospels provided:
Joel 2.1, 2, 12-17 or Isaiah 58.1-12; Psalm 51.1-18; 2 Corinthians

5.20b–6.10; Matthew 6.1-6, 16-21 or John 8.1-11. Some of those who wish to impose ashes as part of the Liturgy of Penitence may find the Matthew reading, with its condemnation of those who disfigure their faces, inappropriate. For them the passage from John, with its stress on sin and forgiveness, will perhaps be more suitable. We should note that the Gospel Acclamation follows the Lenten pattern with no 'alleluias'. A sermon is to be preached, and if the staged rites of the journey towards baptism are to be a part of the local community's observance of Lent, it would seem sensible to explain this here. At least part of the sermon might remind the congregation that the penitential preparation of the whole community is supportive of the catechumens in their pilgrimage of faith and commitment. Whatever you opt for, the Liturgy of the Word, of which the sermon is an important part, should prepare the congregation for the corporate act of penance which comes next.

The Liturgy of Penitence

There are four interlinked elements in this part of the service, one of which is optional. The first is a form of corporate self-examination in litany form of which two examples are provided. This is linked to:

- a general confession – again, two prayers are provided;

- the imposition of ashes, which is the optional element;

- and finally, a presidential prayer where again two forms are provided.

The first litany takes the form of an extended meditation on the second of the standard Prayers of Penitence provided in Order 1. In between its opening confession of sin in 'thought, word and deed' and its concluding petitions for forgiveness and amendment of life comes a series of particular acknowledgements of sin. Some of these may be omitted and others inserted, depending on the pastoral needs of the particular community. As with so many commended texts in *Times and Seasons* there is opportunity here for creativity and responsiveness to circumstance and topicality. This litany is closely based on a Methodist original from the United States.

The second litany is a slightly edited version of parts I to III of the Litany from the *Main Volume* and does not lend itself so well to emendation. However, carefully crafted extra petitions might be added if they were felt to be necessary. This classic litany leads into the first of the authorized confessions in the section of Supplementary Texts of the *Main Volume*.

As neither of the two litany forms provided is mandatory, other forms of self-examination might be used at this point. *Lent, Holy Week and Easter* provided a version of the Ten Commandments at this point which remains highly suitable. The text on pages 270–1 of the *Main Volume* is easily accessible. In the first of its Services of Penitence, *Lent, Holy Week, Easter* also suggested a form of the Beatitudes arranged for self-examination. Again, pastoral circumstances may mean that this is the most appropriate form for use in a particular community. *Common Worship: Christian Initiation* has a useful resource section (pp. 241–53) in its Reconciliation and Restoration section, where all these forms can now be found together with other useful material for this point in the Ash Wednesday service.

Whatever mode of self-examination is chosen, it is vital that there is a significant period of silence before the second element of the Liturgy of Penitence, the confession. Handling periods of silence in liturgy generally requires great care, both at the planning stage and on the part of the president during the service itself. Silence should always appear deliberate and considered, not as if something has gone wrong or the natural flow of the liturgy has been interrupted. Here the conducted examination of conscience should flow into a silence which is significant but not too long and thence into the words of confession, so that the pause is appropriated by each member of the congregation and used to make the confession their own.

The third element in the Liturgy of Penitence is the blessing and imposition of the ashes from which Ash Wednesday takes its name. With or without sackcloth, ashes have been a sign of sorrow, mourning or repentance since biblical times (Esther 4.1; Job 46.2; Jeremiah 6.26; Daniel 9.3; Matthew 11.21 etc.). As the observance of Lent became more elaborate in the early medieval period, with the involvement of the whole congregation not just the catechumens and penitents, the imposition of ashes was seen as an appropriate way to begin a season of repentance and sorrow for sin. *Lent, Holy Week, Easter* formally reintroduced the ceremony to the Church of England in 1986 but it had been observed unofficially in many parishes since the late nineteenth century. If you are teaching about this it may be helpful to focus not just on the biblical significance of ashes in penitence but also on the sign of the cross. As Michael Perham has written, 'The Christian begins Lent by receiving once again the mark of the cross, in dust because of human fallenness, but nevertheless it is the cross, put back where it belongs as the Lent journey to the cross of Christ begins' (*New Handbook of Pastoral Liturgy*, p. 230).

The imposition of ashes is not obligatory and the liturgy can perfectly properly move directly to one of the two presidential prayers provided at the end of this section. If anyone feels uncomfortable with the imposition of ashes there are other means by which individuals can make the corporate act of penitence their own. For example, each member of the congregation could be given a pebble as they come into church which they then bring up and place either at the foot of a cross or add to a small cairn. As individual sins are seen, literally, to pile up, the corporate nature of sin is illustrated.

The ashes used for the imposition need to be prepared carefully in advance. Traditionally they are made from the burnt palm crosses of the previous year. Note 5 preceding the Liturgy of Ash Wednesday suggests that 'Members of the congregation may be asked to return the palm crosses to church on the Sunday before Lent and the palm crosses could be burned as part of the activities of Shrove Tuesday.' Needless to say, the ashes should be cooled, pounded or ground up and passed through a sieve into an appropriate container in order to be ready for use at the liturgy. This should be small enough to hold in one hand, so that the thumb of the right hand can be used to sign a cross on the foreheads of the recipients. The containers of ash can be placed on a small table in front of the president for the blessing.

The prayer said by the president over the ashes is less of a prayer of blessing than a request that in the particular context of Lent the ashes may signify penitence and our mortality. Thus, for those for whom the blessing of inanimate objects presents a problem, there need not be one here.

The president should receive the imposition of ashes first, and then he or she should ash those who are to assist with distributing ash to the congregation. Practically speaking, it is easier to sign the foreheads of those kneeling down rather than standing up and so it may prove best to have the congregation come to the communion rail to kneel and receive the ash. While kneeling may be regarded as a more appropriate posture for an act of penitence than standing, it is also possible to impose ashes on those who come up in single file and stand.

Words to be said to each person are provided for the imposition of ashes but they need not be used. Silence may be kept while the congregation receive the ashes, whether or not the words of imposition are used, and this element of austerity can be very effective in underlining the significance of what is going on. Alternatively a hymn, anthem or psalm may be sung. Psalm 51 is particularly appropriate here if it has not already been used during the Liturgy of the Word or as part of the examination of conscience.

Once all have been ashed, the president may pray one of the two prayers which conclude this part of the liturgy. The two prayers are very different in character. The first is in classical collect shape, as one would expect from a prayer which derives ultimately from the *Gelasian Sacramentary*, and functions as such, very much summing up all that has gone before. It asks indirectly that God will provide the grace needed for us to remain pleasing to him. The second is an authorized absolution from the *Main Volume*, printed in the indicative form but usable in a predicatory way by changing the italicized *you* and *your* into *us* and *our*. As it comes at the end of a serious act of penitence, a prayer of absolution seems more appropriate and if the one provided here, with its overtones of blessing, does not seem quite right then any other from the bank of authorized absolutions may be used.

A final practical point: the president and any others who assisted with the imposition of ashes will want to wash their hands, probably before the Peace if it is to be exchanged, and certainly before the Preparation of the Table. Soap and water and a towel should be provided in some discreet place.

The Liturgy of the Sacrament

Structurally this presents no surprises. Two Prayers at the Preparation of the Table are provided, which are additional to those printed earlier in the Seasonal Material. The Lenten Extended Preface is printed out together with one of the familiar short prefaces from the seasonal resource. There is a suggested form of introduction to the Lord's Prayer provided and also words to be used when the president breaks the consecrated bread. The Prayer after Communion provided for all to say is particularly appropriate at the outset of the Lenten journey and should resonate well with any present who are preparing for baptism at Easter.

The Dismissal

As printed, the conclusion of the service contains one of the new and distinctive features of the *Times and Seasons* provision, the 'dismissal Gospel'. As David Kennedy has explained in more detail in the first volume of this guide, these Gospel passages, proclaimed at the end of a liturgical rite, are designed to strengthen our sense that we are called to *live* the gospel and so to participate both as individuals and as a church in the ongoing work of Christ in the world he came to save. Each of the landmark seasonal services in *Times and Seasons*, be they eucharistic or Services of the Word, provides a recommended dismissal gospel passage, but once the idea has been taken on board other suitable passages may commend themselves locally.

The pattern we have here is a final hymn, an acclamation, the dismissal Gospel (Luke 15.4-7), a solemn or simple blessing, and the dismissal itself. Ideally, the congregation should be encouraged to process during the final hymn to the back of the church, to the space around the font or the area inside the main door, for the dismissal. Here they listen to God's word, receive his blessing and are sent forth to live and work to his praise and glory. The solemn form of blessing is appropriate at the Principal Service of the day and the simple one at any other services that may be pastorally necessary. The extended form of the Dismissal is optional, so the acclamation and the dismissal Gospel may be omitted, leaving just the blessing and dismissal to conclude the service.

Shrove Tuesday

Before moving on from our discussion of Ash Wednesday, it is worth noting that *Common Worship: Daily Prayer* has resources for a Vigil Office which may be used on the evening before Principal Feasts as well as on Saturday evenings. Ash Wednesday is one such Principal Feast. The day before is traditionally known as Shrove Tuesday in England, the day on which the faithful were 'shriven', that is, made their confession and received absolution. Continental names for this day include *Carnaval* (from the Latin, *carne vale* – farewell to meat) or *Mardi Gras* (Fat Tuesday – the day when all non-Lenten foods were used up). The shriving element in Shrove Tuesday may have disappeared in our church life, perhaps it has been replaced by the major focus on penitence on Ash Wednesday, but pancakes still feature on the menu in many households where they represent a farewell to rich food until the feast of Easter. Parishes might like to mark this day with a Vigil Service instead of Evening Prayer and follow the church service with a parish party, perhaps featuring the making and eating of pancakes.

The structure recommended in *Daily Prayer*, suitably adapted, would look like this:

Preparation	*The Blessing of Light*
	Hymn
	Verses from Psalm 141 with refrain
	Opening prayer
The Word of God	*Old Testament reading Genesis 12.14-20*
	New Testament reading Hebrews 12.7-11
	Canticle 67 'A Song of Repentance' with refrain
	Acclamation possibly from Times and Seasons *Lent seasonal material*
	Gospel of Ash Matthew
	Wednesday 6.1-6,16-21
	The Magnificat
Prayers	*Free intercession*
	Collect for Ash Wednesday
	The Lord's Prayer
The Conclusion	*Hymn*
	Concluding versicle and response

The Old and New Testament readings given here are just suggestions. The office readings for the day could be used, although they seem to be wildly inappropriate, or others chosen. The Gospel for Ash Wednesday should always be read. Where there are candidates for baptism at Easter in the community, opportunity should be taken in the intercessions to pray for them as they get ready to begin their final preparation.

The first four Sundays of Lent

One of the great advantages of the freedoms allowed by the notes and instructions attached to the *Common Worship* Holy Communion service and the flexibility inherent in Order One in particular is that the Sunday communion services in each principal liturgical season can be celebrated in a distinctive manner. Thus through a careful consideration of the overall structure and a wise choice of variable texts to clothe it, the character or liturgical 'flavour' of a Lenten Sunday could be made quite different from, say, a Sunday after Christmas or a Sunday in Ordinary Time (after Trinity). Many parishes saw the possibilities of this seasonal differentiation when the *Main Volume* was first published and devised a set of seasonal orders of service for Advent, Christmastide, Lent, Eastertide and Ordinary Time. Now, six years on from the first authorization of the *Common Worship* Holy Communion and with the advent of the extra seasonal resources made available in *Times and Seasons*, these orders could in many cases be profitably revised. Those who have not as yet gone down this road may now feel sufficiently confident with the *Common Worship* material to think of introducing this sort of disciplined variety.

Prayers of Penitence

As the Order One structure page in the *Main Volume* indicates and as the printed order shows, the normative position for the Prayers of Penitence is within the Gathering rite at the beginning of the service. However, note 10 (*Main Volume*, p. 331) allows that 'this section may be transposed to a later point in the service as a response to the Liturgy of the Word'. Lent is a very suitable time to make this transposition. The change will attract the attention of the regular congregation and will give an appropriate added weight to the penitential element in the service. A seasonal invitation to confession could be used and perhaps a different authorized confession from the one used at other times of the year

Alternatively, retaining the penitential element at the beginning of the service, some use could be made of material in the Form of Preparation section in the *Main Volume* which immediately prefaces Order One. The Gathering section of the service thus extended with extra penitential material would mark out the Sundays of Lent as distinctive.

A sadly neglected resource is the Litany. It is included in the *Main Volume* in both its *Common Worship* and *Book of Common Prayer* forms. If your church has the space and the musical resources, an appropriate way of beginning the Lenten Sunday Eucharist is to sing the Litany in procession. You can choose as many petitions as may be needed to cover the required distance, and end up in the chancel with the *Trisagion* or the Kyries, depending on which version is used. The president may then greet the people with 'The Lord be with you, etc.' and introduce the Collect. With this arrangement, the Prayers of Penitence are best said later in the service as a response to the Liturgy of the Word.

Rites on the Way

As discussed earlier, if there are candidates for Christian initiation at Easter the parish may choose to integrate the landmark Rites on the Way into the Sunday liturgy. The proposed pattern places The Call (*Common Worship: Christian Initiation*, pp. 38–9) on the First Sunday of Lent. As prayers of intercession are provided in this first rite it would seem sensible to place it between the recitation of the Creed and the Peace thereby maintaining the usual flow. The Presentation of the Four Texts takes place on each of the subsequent Sundays and the note given in *Common Worship: Christian Initiation* (see pp. 40–7) suggests this is done after the Sermon but, as mentioned above, it can also be done as part of the Dismissal. Common sense suggests that on the Fourth Sunday, when the Apostles' Creed is presented, the regular recitation of the Creed is omitted.

Mothering Sunday

In addition to the three-year cycle of Lent readings, the *Common Worship* Principal Service Lectionary provides a set of alternative readings for those who choose to displace the Fourth Sunday of Lent with the observance of Mothering Sunday, for which there is also a separate collect. This presents liturgy planners with something of a dilemma requiring some pastoral sensitivity. The question is whether to preserve the integrity of Lent with its carefully worked-out lectionary provision or to intrude Mothering Sunday with its wide appeal. One possibility is to consider the brief lessening of austerities, which is traditional on this Refreshment Sunday – rose-coloured vestments and perhaps the blessing and distribution of spring flowers as Mothering Sunday gifts and the serving of simnel cake with coffee after the service.

Those communities nurturing candidates for initiation and walking with them in the Way will most probably choose to preserve the integrity of Lent and at the Principal Service of the day will use the Lent Collect and readings and include the presentation of the Apostles' Creed. A second service during the day, perhaps a Service of the Word, could use the Mothering Sunday provision and thus satisfy those for whom neglect of this celebration would be a serious matter. Communities who are travelling the Lenten journey without candidates for baptism at Easter may not see this as so much of a problem and can opt for the Mothering Sunday provision at their Principal Service.

New Patterns for Worship includes a comprehensive non-sacramental all-age service for Mothering Sunday, with helpful introductory notes including advice on sharing experience of motherhood and the giving of flowers and other gifts (see pp. 416–23). The appointed collect from *Additional Collects* would fit this context well:

> God of love,
> passionate and strong,
> tender and careful:
> watch over us and hold us
> all the days of our life;
> through Jesus Christ our Lord.

There was also a Mothering Sunday section in *Enriching the Christian Year* and it is a pity that some of this material was not included in *Times and Seasons*. In particular, the following sections would provide helpful resources:

> *Invitations to Confession*
>> Jesus said,
>> Before you offer your gift, go and be reconciled.
>> As brothers and sisters in God's family,
>> we come together to ask his forgiveness.
>
> *(or)*
>
>> We have done what was wrong in the Lord's sight
>> and chosen what displeased him.
>> Yet as a mother comforts her child,
>> so shall the Lord himself comfort us.

So let us come to him who knows our every deed and
thought.

Kyrie Confession

As a father is tender towards his children,
so is the Lord tender to those that fear him:
Lord, have mercy.
Lord, have mercy.

He will not always be chiding,
nor will he keep his anger for ever:
Christ, have mercy.
Christ, have mercy.

I have calmed and quieted my soul,
like a child upon its mother's breast is my soul within me:
Lord, have mercy.
Lord, have mercy.

Intercessions

We pray for the family of the Church and for the life of
families around us, saying
Father of all
hear your children's prayer.

Sovereign Lord, your Son has revealed you as our
heavenly Father, from whom every family in heaven and
on earth is named . . .
Father of all
hear your children's prayer.

You have made your Church a spiritual family, a
household of faith. Through baptism we are reborn as
the brothers and sisters of Christ. Deepen our unity and
fellowship in him . . .
Father of all
hear your children's prayer.

You sent your Son to give his life as a ransom for the whole
human family. Give justice, peace and racial harmony to
the world he died to save . . .
Father of all
hear your children's prayer.

You gave your Son a share in the life of a family in Nazareth.
Help us to value our families, to be thankful for them, and
to live sensitively within them . . .
Father of all
hear your children's prayer.

Your Son drew around him a company of friends. Bring
love and joy to all who are alone. Help us all to find in
the brothers and sisters of Christ a loving family . . .
Father of all
hear your children's prayer.

You are the God of the dead as well as of the living. In
confidence we remember those of the household of
faith who have gone before us . . . Bring us with them to
the joy of your home in heaven, where you are alive and
reign now and for ever.
Amen.

(or)

For all mothers and fathers,
Lord, receive our thanks and prayer.

For the security of homes and family life,
Lord, receive our thanks and prayer.

For the joy of all loving human relationships,
Lord, receive our thanks and prayer.

For your holy catholic Church, the mother of
us all,
Lord, receive our thanks and prayer.

For your family in this place, and our life together,
Lord, receive our thanks and prayer.

For all the members of our families who have died,
and now find their home in you,
Lord, receive our thanks and prayer.

For Mary, the Mother of Jesus,
and for all who seek to follow her example of
motherhood,
Lord, receive our thanks and prayer.

Introduction to the Peace

Jesus said,
'Whoever does the will of God
is my brother, and sister and mother.'
As we have opportunity, let us work for good to all,
especially to members of the household of faith.

Prefaces

And now we give you thanks
because your eternal Word took our nature upon him
in the womb of Mary the Virgin.
The sword of sorrow pierced her heart
when he was lifted high on the cross,
and by his sacrifice made our peace with you.
Therefore . . .

(or)

And now we give you thanks
because in his earthly childhood
you entrusted him to the care of a human family.
In Mary and Joseph you give us
an example of love and devotion to him,
and also a pattern of family life.
Therefore . . .

Simple blessing

May the Father from whom every family
in earth and heaven receives its name
strengthen you with his Spirit in your inner being
so that Christ may dwell in your hearts by faith
(and that, knowing his love,
broad and long, deep and high beyond all knowledge,
you may be filled with all the fullness of God);
and the blessing. . .

Extended blessing

When the Word became flesh
earth was joined to heaven in the womb of Mary:
may the love and obedience of Mary
be your example.
Amen.

May the peace of Christ
rule in your hearts and homes.
Amen.

May you be filled with the joys of the Spirit
and the gifts of your eternal home.
Amen.

And the blessing . . .

Michael Vasey's fine version of a Song of Anselm from *Common Worship: Daily Prayer* (p. 639) would find a natural setting on this day:

Jesus, like a mother you gather your people to you;
you are gentle with us as a mother with her children.

Often you weep over our sins and our pride,
tenderly you draw us from hatred and judgement.

You comfort us in sorrow and bind up our wounds,
in sickness you nurse us, and with pure milk you feed us.

Jesus, by your dying we are born to new life;
by your anguish and labour we come forth in joy.

Despair turns to hope through your sweet goodness;
through your gentleness we find comfort in fear.

Your warmth gives life to the dead,
your touch makes sinners righteous.

Lord Jesus, in your mercy heal us;
in your love and tenderness remake us.

In your compassion bring grace and forgiveness,
for the beauty of heaven may your love prepare us.

The Way of the Cross

The Way of the Cross or Stations of the Cross, to give the more traditional title, is a time-honoured and popular devotion for many Christians, especially during Lent and Passiontide. Some of the historical background is set out on page 236 of *Times and Seasons*.

However, for some Anglicans the fact that the traditional stations (as set out on page 256 of *Times and Seasons*) have included non-biblical and legendary elements (e.g. Jesus falling three times and St Veronica wiping the face of Jesus) has proved difficult. Therefore, the growing popularity over recent years of schemes of biblical stations is a welcome ecumenical development, and *Times and Seasons* provides one such scheme of 15 stations, all of which are drawn from the passion narratives of the Gospels. The 15 stations are:

1. Jesus in agony in the Garden of Gethsemane
2. Jesus betrayed by Judas and arrested
3. Jesus condemned by the Sanhedrin
4. Peter denies Jesus
5. Jesus judged by Pilate
6. Jesus scourged and crowned with thorns
7. Jesus carries the cross
8. Simon of Cyrene helps Jesus to carry the cross
9. Jesus meets the women of Jerusalem
10. Jesus is crucified
11. Jesus promises the kingdom to the penitent thief
12. Jesus on the cross; his mother and his friend
13. Jesus dies on the cross
14. Jesus laid in the tomb
15. Jesus risen from the dead.

Each station includes

- a responsory
- a reading
- a reflection/meditation
- a prayer.

The Notes on page 237 give helpful suggestions about how this material may be used. Many, of course, will wish to use it in the

42

traditional way: a semi-formal procession around the stations, pausing at each one for a reading, a reflection and prayer. Note 1 gives advice on the use of images. Many publishers and diocesan resource centres will stock suitable images, although at present most will be for the traditional stations. However, it is perfectly possible for churches to make their own, perhaps by running an art group or, again as note 1 suggests, by using symbols to represent the various stations.

Note 2 stresses the desirability of movement. Of course, not all of the stations need to be used at once; one church spread the devotion over three evening services on Monday, Tuesday, and Wednesday of Holy Week. This was more suited to the rather cramped church building, but also gave time for silence and singing at each station as well as a short meditation. Projecting images of the passion is another possibility where resources allow.

Note 4 sets out the variety of possibilities for response, including penitence, praise, intercession or some action. This could supplement or replace the prayers provided in the order.

Note 5 comments on music, including the traditional use of *Stabat Mater* ('At the cross her station keeping', *New English Hymnal* 97, *Common Praise* 104). However, the various stations give scope for the use of devotional hymns and songs, or for anthems and motets where there is a choir.

Note 6 gives advice if the Way of the Cross is combined with Holy Communion.

Festivals

Finally, it is worth noting that *Common Worship: Festivals* includes full provision for St Joseph's Day (19 March, see pp. 47–51) and the Feast of the Annunciation (25 March, see pp. 52–6). Depending on the date of Easter, both could fall either in Lent or in Eastertide (transferred) – see Calendar Rules, *Festivals*, p. 25.

3 Passiontide and Holy Week

> The royal banners forward go,
> the cross shines forth in mystic glow;
> where he in flesh, our flesh who made,
> our sentence bore, our ransom paid.
> *Venantius Fortunatus (tr. J. M. Neale)*

The wondrous cross

The cross of Jesus, of course, stands at the very heart of our faith. We echo the warm and deeply personal words of St Paul:

> I have been crucified with Christ; and it is no longer I who live, but it is Christ who lives in me. And the life I now live in the flesh I live by faith in the Son of God, who loved me and gave himself for me.
>
> *Galatians 2.19, 20*

While the cross must be central to our worship throughout the year, Passiontide and Holy Week give us the opportunity to meditate directly and unhurriedly on Jesus' sacrifice of himself for us and for our salvation. Passiontide and Holy Week are still part of Lent, and throughout Lent there is a growing sense of moving towards the crisis of the passion. The Fifth Sunday in Lent marks a significant gear change, as we focus specifically on the cross and its meaning. So the appointed collects for Lent 5 reflect this transition:

> Most merciful God,
> who by the death and resurrection of your Son Jesus Christ
> delivered and saved the world;
> grant that by faith in him who suffered on the cross
> we may triumph in the power of his victory;
> through Jesus Christ your Son our Lord . . .
> *(Main Volume,* p. 396)
>
> Gracious Father,
> you gave up your Son
> out of love for the world:
> lead us to ponder the mysteries of his passion,
> that we may know eternal peace
> through the shedding of our Saviour's blood,
> Jesus Christ our Lord. *(Additional Collects,* p.13)

But note that it is a holistic spirituality; as the Introduction to the
Season makes clear (*Times and Seasons*, p. 259), the primitive Christian
Pascha embraced both Christ's death *and* resurrection as a celebration
of salvation. Bishop Kenneth Stevenson has helpfully categorized this
as a 'unitive' piety. So, at the beginning of Passiontide, we are invited to
look at the cross in the light of the resurrection and the gift of salvation.
In this way, the readings appointed in the Principal Service Lectionary
act as a kind of backcloth for the following two weeks:

Year A

Ezekiel 37.1-14: the valley of the dry bones – from death to
    resurrection
Psalm 130: from the darkness of *de profundis* to the promise of
    'plenteous redemption'
Romans 8.6-11: from spiritual death to life in the Spirit, the Spirit who
    raised the Lord Jesus from death
John 11.1-45: the raising of Lazarus by the Resurrection and the Life
    – from tears to joy

Year B

Jeremiah 31.31-34: the promise of a new covenant
Psalm 51.1-13: the reality of sin and the plea for deliverance
or Psalm 119.9-16: trust in God's word
Hebrews 5.5-10: Jesus who learned obedience through suffering and so
    became the source of eternal salvation

45

John 12.20-33: the glorification of the Son of Man, who will draw all people to himself

Year C

Isaiah 43.16-21: 'I am about to do a new thing'

Psalm 126: 'those who sow in tears shall reap with songs of joy'

Philippians 3.4b-14: 'I want to know Christ and the power of his resurrection and the sharing of his sufferings'

John 12.1-8: the anointing at Bethany for the day of Christ's burial

This holistic spirituality is an important insight before we begin to engage with the unfolding story of the passion in Holy Week and imaginatively enter into the drama of the week of the passion.

Passion Sunday?

Anglicans of an older generation will be used to calling the Fifth Sunday in Lent 'Passion Sunday'. However, the title 'Passion Sunday' never appears in *Common Worship*. This is partly because the Roman Catholic liturgical reforms following the Second Vatican Council eliminated 'passiontide' as such from the Roman Catholic calendar. This was to avoid any suggestion that 'passiontide' is a separate 'season'; on the contrary, it is an integral part of the Lenten season which extends from Ash Wednesday to Easter Eve. So, in the Roman Calendar, the first five Sundays are Sundays of Lent and the sixth Sunday is designated as 'Palm Sunday of the Passion of Christ', although the official Roman documents also confusingly refer to Lent 6 as 'Passion Sunday (Palm Sunday)'.

Common Worship also designates the first five Sundays as 'Sundays of Lent', but retains the term 'Passiontide' to designate the period from the Fifth Sunday in Lent to Easter Eve, so embracing the majority of Holy Week; as *Common Worship: Daily Prayer* expresses it:

> Although Passiontide is part of Lent, material proper to Passiontide is used from Evening Prayer on the Eve of the Fifth Sunday in Lent to the evening of Easter Eve (p. xix).

So while there is officially no 'Passion Sunday' as such, the Anglican retention of Lent 6 as 'Palm Sunday' means that the older usage of Passion Sunday for Lent 5 is likely to continue as a piece of shorthand!

Seasonal material

The Seasonal Material (*Times and Seasons*, pp. 260–7) provides the accustomed enrichment material for the Eucharist and a Service of the Word.

Invitation to Confession Two forms are provided: the first, drawing on Romans 5.8, is from the *Main Volume* Seasonal Provisions for Passiontide (*Main Volume*, pp. 312–13), and the second, adapted from 1 Peter 2.24, was written by David Silk.

Kyrie Confession The first form draws on verses from one of the great psalms used in Christian liturgy at Passiontide, Psalm 69, and the second is an imaginative devotion based on the story of Jesus' betrayal and Peter's denials:

Lord Jesus Christ,
we confess that we have failed you as did your first disciples.
We ask for your mercy and help.

When we take our ease
rather than watch with you:
Lord, forgive us.
Christ have mercy.

When we bestow a kiss of peace
yet nurse enmity in our hearts:
Lord, forgive us.
Christ have mercy.

When we strike at those who hurt us
rather than stretch out our hands to bless:
Lord, forgive us.
Christ have mercy.

When we deny that we know you
for fear of the world and its scorn:
Lord, forgive us.
Christ have mercy.

A complementary text is given in *New Patterns for Worship* (p. 76):

> We watch at a distance,
> and are slow to follow Christ in the way of the cross.
> Lord, have mercy.
> **Lord, have mercy.**
>
> We warm our hands by the fire,
> and are afraid to be counted among his disciples.
> Christ, have mercy.
> **Christ, have mercy.**
>
> We run away,
> and fail to share the pain of Christ's suffering.
> Lord, have mercy.
> **Lord, have mercy.**

Gospel Acclamation From the *Main Volume* Seasonal Propers, drawing on Philippians 2.8, 9.

Intercessions Three forms are provided, the first from *Lent, Holy Week and Easter*, and the other forms from *Enriching*.

Introductions to the Peace The first form, based on Ephesians 2.13,14, is from the *Main Volume* Seasonal Provisions. The second form, also adapted from material in Ephesians 2, is from the bank of Introductions to the Peace in Holy Communion: Supplementary Texts (*Main Volume*, p. 290).

Prayer at the Preparation of the Table A new text, drawing on the Johannine imagery of Jesus as the bread of life and the true vine:

> Jesus, true vine and bread of life,
> ever giving yourself that the world might live,
> let us share your death and passion:
> make us perfect in your love.
> **Amen.**

Prefaces Two short Prefaces are provided: the first from the *Main Volume* Seasonal Provisions; the second, adapted from John 12.32 and Hebrews 5.9, from *ASB* Rite A.

48

Extended Preface Taken from the *President's Edition*, this is a new text, inspired by material from the *Roman Missal* and drawing on the text of a short preface from *Enriching*.

Blessings The short form of the blessing is from the *Main Volume* Seasonal Provisions, while the extended formula is from the *President's Edition*.

Short Passages of Scripture Three are provided from Lamentations 1, John 12 and Galatians 6; the second would be particularly suitable at the Preparation of the Gifts, and the third as a post-communion sentence or concluding text in A Service of the Word.

Holy Week

For many Christians, Holy Week is the richest, most moving and spiritually most challenging week of the whole year. Where it is observed with thought and care, it can be means of genuine renewal in discipleship and outreach.

There is a rich and diverse tradition of Anglican creativity in how churches approach the 'Great Week', to give it its fourth-century Jerusalem title. There is no substitute for forward planning and team-work. Too often in the past, the approach to Holy Week worship has depended on, or been left to, the imagination and energy (or lack of it) of the vicar!

Where a church ministry team, worship group, PCC or specially appointed group is able to pray and plan and share both imagination and practical tasks, the results can be magnificent. Some questions that might be asked well in advance are:

- What pattern of services should be adopted in a single church building or group of churches?

- What provision is made for children and young people?

- What evangelistic opportunities does the week provide?

- Is any aspect of the celebration in public places?

- Is there any ecumenical potential?

- How can music, drama and other visual arts be used?

- How can the *Times and Seasons* materials be used or adapted?

- Does there need to be any specific teaching, for example during Lent, to enable congregations to engage with the liturgical provision?

- Practically, what do we need to purchase for the celebration?

- How might the church building be decorated in Holy Week and for Easter?

Holy Week marks a shift from the more 'unitive' approach we noted earlier regarding Lent 5 (see p. 45). Now, we begin to engage with the story as a chronology. In doing so, we follow the gospel chronology first used in fourth-century Jerusalem, where the scheme was:

Saturday: 'Lazarus Saturday', commemorating the anointing at Bethany, John 12.1 ('Six days before the Passover', i.e. reckoning the Passover as beginning Thursday evening)

Sunday: commemoration of the entry into Jerusalem (John 12.12, 'the next day')

Thursday: commemoration of the arrest in the garden and trial

Friday: commemoration of the crucifixion (the day of preparation for the Sabbath)

Saturday evening – Sunday:
the great Vigil of Easter (the first day of the week)

However, this spirituality is not a pretence that the resurrection 'has not yet happened'. For example, the petition of the Collect for Palm Sunday and the first half of Holy Week asks

> grant that we may follow the example of his patience and
> humility,
> and also be made partakers of his resurrection;
> through Jesus Christ your Son our Lord,
> who is alive and reigns . . .

But there is a strong spiritual dynamic of walking with Christ in his sufferings and imaginatively entering into the story of his passion. A particular resource here is the great Passion Narratives of the four gospels, which themselves have their own particular theological emphases. These narratives take up a large proportion of each gospel, a sure sign of the importance of the story for the evangelists and earliest Christian communities.

'Paschal Triduum'

If 'Passiontide' is a particular period within Lent, then Lent comes to a conclusion with the observance of what the Roman Rite calls the Easter Triduum (three days), beginning with the Liturgy of Maundy Thursday, embracing the Liturgy of Good Friday, and concluding with the Easter Vigil and the first Eucharist of Easter. This is the Christian Passover, drawing for its spirituality on the primitive 'unitive' vigil rite of the Early Church, and informed by the great themes of Passover. It is helpful to see the principal services of Maundy Thursday, Good Friday and Easter Day as a continuum, a single rite spread over three days:

- the Liturgy of Maundy Thursday: adjourned, continuing with . . .

- the Liturgy of Good Friday: adjourned, continuing with . . .

- the Easter Vigil or principal Easter celebration.

This understanding enables Christian people to see the importance of observing *all three parts* as an integrated celebration. The evening Liturgy of Maundy Thursday begins the spirituality, taken over from the Passover liturgy, of 'This is the night . . .'; this understanding then continues in the 'darkness' of Good Friday ('and there was darkness over the whole land') and culminates in the joyful strains of 'This is the night' in the *Exsultet* of the Easter Vigil. I expressed this understanding in a Maundy Thursday sermon preached at Durham Cathedral in 2007:

> The joyful and florid cadences of the words 'This is the night', sung at the Easter Vigil, seem to be on *this night* an eternity away. Never in human and Christian experience is there as much space between a Thursday and a Sunday as in these days. But the phrase 'This is the night' is as meaningful for this evening as it will be on the dawning splendour of Sunday morning.
>
> For in the Church's liturgical imagination, what we begin tonight is a single sequence, a single integrated celebration of the Lord's passion and resurrection. The sequence begins tonight and is, as it were, adjourned; it continues at 12 noon tomorrow with the Liturgy of Good Friday and is again adjourned. It then continues

with the great Vigil of Easter and the celebration is brought to glorious completion. And behind it all is the spirituality of the Jewish Passover, commemorating *the night* when God began his great act of deliverance and salvation, bringing his people from slavery to freedom, from despair to joy, from death to life. The great Passover meal, eaten in conformity to the law, at night, was the setting of Jesus' Last Supper with his disciples in the Synoptic Gospels, and at least in its imagery in the Fourth Gospel also. This is the night, a darkness that we enter this evening and a darkness that remains – for even at the height of the sun's strength – noon on Friday – there was darkness over the whole land. It is a darkness we enter; it is a darkness we must confront. A night that must envelop us.

The Fourth Gospel, in simple yet utterly profound language, tells us that at the supper, when Judas Iscariot received the sop, he went out and it was night; the power of darkness at its most utterly dark. This is the night.

And in encountering this night, this darkness, there is a tremendous sense of cost. For to overcome this darkness, to banish night, required the total and absolute self-offering of the Son of God, even to death, the death of the cross.

So, at the Last Supper, the words of Jesus, 'This is my body, given for you; this is my blood, poured out for you and for many for the remission of sins', are words of utter consecration: my *self*, my *life*, given, poured out, given, given to the uttermost, surrendered, offered, for the sake of the world and its salvation.

And the footwashing – no mere theatre; not even simply an exemplar of loving service, although it is that – but as with the Eucharist, another utterly powerful sign of what the cross would achieve – a costly cleaning; not merely the removal of dust and grime from dirty Jerusalem streets, but the inward and spiritual cleansing that makes possible the word of grace – 'you are clean'.

And the great prayer of John 17, so rightly called 'The Prayer of Consecration', an agony of intercession, on the basis of Christ's 'yes' to the Father's will, for the disciples, for their protection, for their unity, for those who will believe, and again for their unity.

And the agony in the garden, the spiritual battle raging between love and evil, obedience and disobedience; a human battle raging within Jesus himself, bone of our bone and flesh of our flesh, and a cosmic battle raging in the heavenlies: 'And there was war in heaven', as the Book of Revelation so graphically and fearfully states it.

And the cost of desertion, denial, injustice, false witness, mockery and all the rest of the narrative of this night; the naked outpouring of darkness when it is utterly dark, what human beings, what we, in our rebellion and evil, do to God, how we respond to perfect love.

There is a wonderful graciousness in God. We participate, whether actually or imaginatively, in the footwashing and we are cleansed. We receive the eucharistic gifts and we are fed; the cost Christ bore is applied to us. We become part of the fruit of his passion. But, in case that sounds just too easy, too presumptive, we can't evade the night, the darkness. We mustn't evade it or nothing wonderful will happen this Easter.

Maundy Thursday in part always leaves me troubled. 'A new commandment I give to you, that you love one another; as I have loved you, so you must love one another.' 'Father, may they all be one, that the world might believe.'

And here we are, in our tribal denominational or tradition-based groups, with our wretched rules and 'integrities', excommunicating and excommunicated, parading our divisions, and very often our rank lack of charity, *caritas* – an offence to the *ubi caritas et amor, Deus ibi est* – 'where charity and love are – there is God' – the great anthem of Maundy Thursday. So the aching absence of God in our uncharitableness which renders the Church impotent to speak prophetically to a world which itself divides and oppresses, unable ever to forgive and to forget; a church and a world which collude with the night, which enjoy the darkness and allow themselves to become seduced and corrupted by it.

Which is why, as always, tonight needs to begin with each of us. As we are confronted anew by the love of Christ which embraced such cost, and celebrate it in sacramental signs, the issue for us is this.

This is the night in which things in us must die, because they mustn't be allowed to continue to live. By that I mean the attitudes, the prejudices, the stored resentments, the repeated and persistent sins, the chips on the shoulder, the withheld absolutions. These are things for which Christ died; indeed, the things which crucified him. These are things for which he offers cleansing; these are the things of death that must be overcome by life, the things of slavery from which we need to be liberated, if this night is to be a night of salvation.

And I don't pretend it's easy. For we enjoy our store of wrong attitudes, we nurse our chips on the shoulder, we carefully file the memories and words that we can bring out as weapons.

Which is why this is the night, in which we may need to struggle, as Christ himself struggled in Gethsemane, until we can take all these things to where they rightly belong, and nail them to the cross, and leave them in Christ's tomb, dead, impotent, sorted.

Only if in these days we confront the night – the night within as well as the night without – can this darkness be turned to light. And then, in dawning glory, the joyful and florid cadences of 'this is the night' will ring out – 'night truly blessed, because sin has been put to flight'.

'Judas when he had received the sop went out, and it was night.'

It's getting dark. We all, individually, have work to do. How shall we confront this darkness? For this is the night.

The Liturgy of Palm Sunday

Times and Seasons provides a fully worked-out text for this day. It is a light revision of that in *Lent, Holy Week, Easter*, itself a recognition of how successfully that provision has taken root in the Church of England. For the record, the changes are:

- a fuller form of presidential greeting is given

- a bidding is provided before the Collect

- the collect from *Additional Collects* is included as an alternative

- the Passiontide acclamation is provided before the reading of the Gospel

- the 'Once you were far off . . .' form is used for the Peace

- the Passiontide prayer at the Preparation of the Table is used

- the Passiontide extended preface is provided

- the 1 Corinthians 11 form of words at the breaking of the bread is given

- the *Common Worship* presidential post-communion prayer is substituted for the *Lent, Holy Week, Easter* form (the collect for Lent 3, *ASB* and *CW*)

- a new congregational post-communion prayer is provided, from *The Book of Alternative Services* (Canada)

- the Passiontide extended blessing is given.

The structure (*Times and Seasons*, p. 268) sets out clearly the fourfold nature of this rite with the main headings:

- Commemoration of the Lord's Entry into Jerusalem

- The Liturgy of the Word

- The Liturgy of the Sacrament

- The Dismissal

The *Times and Seasons* text simply sets out the basic textual framework; how it is presented gives scope for imagination and creativity.

Commemoration of the Lord's Entry into Jerusalem

This part of the rite has the following structure

- Anthem/acclamation

- Greeting

- Introduction (text or other appropriate words)

- Prayer over the palms or branches

- Palm Gospel
- The Procession
- The Collect

Note 1 (p. 268) suggests that for the procession, the congregation should assemble apart from the church building, in the open air or in a church hall or other suitable place. Or that the procession should be around or within the church building. Obviously, wise local decisions need to be made.

A public procession from a suitable place can be dramatic and meaningful as well as providing a 'public' element to the rite. Considerations will include:

- What is an acceptable distance?
- What about elderly, infirm or disabled members of the congregation?
- Are there issues of road safety?
- Have any necessary permissions been sought for a potentially large outdoor procession?
- What about issues of audibility?
- Who will provide the music?
- What about a wet weather contingency?

Whatever the case, the tone of the procession is joyful, characterized by the word 'hosanna', which derives from the Hebrew as a plea, 'O Lord, save us' (Psalm 118.25), but which in time became a shout of joyful acclamation especially associated with that most joyful of Jewish festivals, the Feast of Tabernacles. The Palm Sunday procession should be markedly different from the traditionally sober Good Friday marches of witness.

For that reason, note 2 suggests that palms or other branches should be used. Branches of palm, olive, myrtle and citron were traditionally waved as a sign of joy in procession at Tabernacles, and the Gospel accounts state that people cut down branches when Jesus entered Jerusalem (Mark 11.8). It is difficult to create this sense of celebration with traditional palm crosses, so there is something to be said either for members of the congregation to bring their own branches or for some judicious spring pruning in the church grounds or vicarage garden! Again, health and safety concerns will seek to ensure that branches can be waved safely, especially in confined spaces.

It is worth noting that the prayer over the palms or branches is not strictly a *blessing*. Rather, the branches are held up as a sign of Christ's victory and symbol of our following in his way. Where actual branches are used, but receiving a palm cross is also valued or expected, these can be distributed without ceremony at the end of the service. They should be seen as a sign of Christ's love and sacrifice, not as 'lucky charms'.

Two examples illustrate some of the possibilities for this part of the rite.

In St Paul's parish, there were three Christian churches in the High Street – Anglican, Roman Catholic and Methodist. The local Churches Together had established a long-standing tradition of shared worship in Holy Week, including a march of witness on Good Friday and a dawn service on Easter Day. The three churches also began Holy Week with a shared commemoration on Palm Sunday. While all three held their usual main Sunday service at different times, they agreed to meet on Palm Sunday at 10am in the local park. A brass ensemble was booked to play. As the congregations arrived, palm crosses were distributed. As the rite of the Commemoration of the Lord's Entry into Jerusalem was so similar in the *Roman Missal*, *Times and Seasons* and *The Methodist Worship Book* (see pp. 236–9), a joint rite was quickly agreed. A group of singers from the three churches provided a strong choir. After the blessing of palms and the palm gospel, the procession set off, accompanied by the band, with the singing of 'All glory, laud and honour', and then the song 'Sing Hosanna'. The band and choir were placed in the middle of the procession to enable maximum participation from the congregation. In the forecourt of the Roman Catholic Church, the Peace was exchanged, and then the congregations divided for the Eucharist, the Anglicans and Methodists holding a joint celebration in one of their two churches. While there was sadness that the three congregations could not share in the Eucharist, there was also a strong sense of unity and fellowship which transcended denominational conventions.

At St Stephen's, Palm Sunday was always a highlight of the year, not least for the children, because one of the local farmers loaned a donkey, which he carefully supervised. Before the service, a group of parishioners cut down about 200 branches for the large congregation, which included the uniformed organizations on their 'parade' Sunday. The commemoration took place in the hall forecourt or, in wet weather, within the church hall itself. The music group, including guitars and brass, provided the music. The Sunday school had made paper 'palm branches', painted in brown and green, which avoided safety concerns about the use of real branches by children. After a welcome and greeting, the Palm Sunday story was enacted by the youth group. The procession then made its way to the parish church, with the exuberant waving of branches and joyful singing. It made quite an impact on passers-by!

In church, a number of elderly and infirm members of the congregation had felt unable to participate in the procession, so a parallel commemoration was led by the Reader.

The procession included the singing of a series of joyful worship songs, including 'Make way', 'Hosanna in the highest' and 'Come on and celebrate'. At the church door, the branches were laid down and as the ministers entered, the hymn 'Ride on, ride on' completely changed the atmosphere from triumphant praise to serious contemplation of the passion.

The Liturgy of the Word

One set of readings is provided for all three years for the readings before the Gospel: Isaiah 50.4-9a, Psalm 31.9-16, [17, 18], and Philippians 2.5-11. The Gospel reading is:

Year A   Matthew 26.14–27.66 or Matthew 27.11-54
Year B   Mark 14.1–15.47 or 15.1-39, [40-47]
Year C   Luke 22.14–23.56 or 23.1-49

There is a widespread tradition of reading the Gospel as a dramatic reading. Note 3 states that the Gospel 'may be read or sung by three or more people', an allusion to the medieval sung passions, with a tenor singing the part of the Evangelist, a bass Jesus, and an alto the other single voices, with the choir singing the 'group' parts. *Proclaiming the Passion: The Passion narratives in dramatized form* (Church House Publishing) was produced in 2007 as a *Common Worship* resource for Holy Week. Dramatized versions can also be found in *Lent, Holy Week and Easter* and *The Dramatized Bible*, as well as other publications. The Introduction to *Proclaiming the Passion* (pp. 1–3) gives comprehensive advice on staging a dramatized reading, as well as suggestions for employing images and music, and advice on posture. For example, it says this on 'images and music':

> Where facilities and layout allow, a projected sequence of images can greatly enhance the reading. Images should be carefully selected so as to support the text rather than work against it. As a general rule, they should aim to provide an evocative backdrop to the words, rather than try to be interpretative. Music might also be used as a background to at least some of the reading, though this needs exceptionally careful planning and preparation.

If a dramatized reading is contemplated, rehearsal is essential if the power of the narrative is to be communicated well.

It will be noted that while the Palm Gospel includes the customary congregational gospel responses, the Passion Gospel on Palm Sunday and Good Friday has no such response. This is an illustration of a change in emphasis. As noted above, 'Ride on, ride on' is an excellent transition from the praise of the procession to the contemplation of Christ's suffering. This accords with the whole spirituality of the rite: entering the church building becomes a dramatic symbol of entering the city with Christ, where we know that the 'Hosannas' will turn to 'Crucify him' and we shall see the ambiguities of our own discipleship exposed. So there is an austerity and reflectiveness in the rest of the service. On entering the church, the Collect of the Day sets out the great truth of the cross:

Almighty and everlasting God,
who in your tender love towards the human race
    sent your Son our Saviour Jesus Christ
to take upon him our flesh
and to suffer death upon the cross . . .

In the readings we reflect on prophecy, St Paul's great hymn of Philippians 2 and then we hear and participate in the story. Not everyone finds the invitation to join in the shouts of the crowd to be comfortable – some, indeed, regard it as inappropriate – but we should expect different responses and different standpoints. The intercession from *Lent, Holy Week and Easter* has been crafted with great skill; our response, 'Lord, have mercy', concluded by the *Trisagion*, relates the way of the cross to the harsh realities of human life and the shortfalls of Christian discipleship.

Times and Seasons makes provision for a sermon, but where the full provision is used for the Palm Sunday liturgy, some will feel that the Liturgy of the Palms and the Liturgy of the Word with its long Passion Gospel are their own sermon. One possibility is for a short comment or reflection to be used after both Gospel readings. The other consideration is the place of silence – it is certainly most appropriate and effective at the end of the Passion Gospel.

The Liturgy of the Sacrament

This is straightforward, but thought should be given as to which Eucharistic Prayer is used. Prayer C seems particularly fitting, with its Cranmerian emphasis on the cross, but would not be used with the extended preface.

The Dismissal

Again follows the normal pattern. In some churches, the Kenyan blessing is used effectively; the text is set out thus in *New Patterns* (p. 303):

The congregation accompanies the first three responses with a sweep of the arm towards a cross, as if throwing the objects of the prayer; the final response is a sweep of the arm towards heaven.

All our problems
we send to the cross of Christ.

All our difficulties
we send to the cross of Christ.

All the devil's works
we send to the cross of Christ.

All our hopes
we set on the risen Christ;
and the blessing . . .

Where palm crosses have been distributed, they are held up for the dismissal; an Iona text is popular:

The Cross . . .
We shall take it.

The bread . . .
We shall break it.

The pain . . .
We shall bear it.

The joy . . .
We shall share it.

The gospel . . .
We shall live it.

The love . . .
We shall give it.

The light . . .
We shall cherish it.

The darkness . . .
God shall perish it.

Of course, some churches will prefer a much simpler style of service, perhaps drawing either on the Liturgy of Palms or the Liturgy of the Passion. Others will use material from the Passiontide bank, have an all-age service, or celebrate Morning Prayer or A Service of the Word. An excellent non-eucharistic all-age approach to Palm Sunday is found in *Together for a Season* (pp. 88–100).

Similarly, a church holding a second service, for example in the evening, will draw on further resources. In times past, the RSCM devotion *The Cross of Christ* was hugely popular; in 2007 a new resource, *The Way of the Cross: A Passiontide Sequence*, was published, compiled by David Ogden and Peter Moger and based on the Way of the Cross material from *Times and Seasons*. This of course could be used at any suitable time in Passiontide.

Monday, Tuesday, Wednesday in Holy Week

Times and Seasons does not include any specific material for these days; in many churches a daily Eucharist will be celebrated, where the appointed Gospel reading for all three years takes up the Johannine narrative:

Monday:	John 12.1-12	The anointing at Bethany
Tuesday:	John 12.20-36	The request of the Greeks for a meeting with Jesus: 'The hour has come for the Son of Man to be glorified'
Wednesday:	John 13.21-32	'One of you will betray me . . .'

Alternatively, some will value using the lections appointed in *The Book of Common Prayer*, with Gospel readings from the Synoptic passion narratives:

Monday:	Mark 14.1-72
Tuesday:	Mark 15.1-39
Wednesday:	Luke 22.1-71

There are many liturgical possibilities for the first half of Holy Week apart from the Eucharist, including

- Evening Prayer, *BCP* or *CW: Daily Prayer* (pp. 257–62)

- Address and Compline (*Main Volume*, pp. 81–99; *Daily Prayer*, pp. 333–43, see especially the Passiontide material on p. 352)

- The Way of the Cross (*Times and Seasons*, pp. 236–56)

- Tenebrae ('Darkness'), see, for example, the form in *The Book of Occasional Services* 2003 of the Episcopal Church of the USA or, in a more simple form, *The United Methodist Book of Worship* (USA)

- a short daily devotional service of readings, prayers and Passiontide music

- short acts of worship led by home groups or other groups in the church.

At St Andrew's Church, the long established home groups, which normally met for Bible study and prayer, were invited to devise and present a short act of worship for the first three evenings in Holy Week. During Lent, the groups prepared the acts of worship, reflecting on different aspects of the story of the passion. The services were a great enrichment to the worshipping life of the church, always creatively presented and enabling diverse gifts to be used and developed.

Another *Common Worship: Daily Prayer* resource is Prayers at the Foot of the Cross (see pp. 317–18), which can form the conclusion of a daily act of worship.

Maundy Thursday

Times and Seasons provides three blocks of material: Resources for a Chrism Eucharist (pp. 278–91), The Reception of Holy Oils during the Liturgy of Maundy Thursday (p. 292), and The Liturgy of Maundy Thursday (pp. 293–304.)

Resources for a Chrism Eucharist

This is a bank of material for use at an episcopally led service, usually in the cathedral during the day on Maundy Thursday or on an earlier occasion in Holy Week. Most dioceses have their own particular approach to this rite, under the direction of the bishop. An excellent historical note (*Times and Seasons*, p. 278) gives the necessary background and major biblical and theological themes.

The Reception of Holy Oils during the Liturgy of Maundy Thursday

This short rite, forming part of the Gathering of The Liturgy of Maundy Thursday, makes explicit the link between the diocesan

Chrism Eucharist and the use of oils in the regular worshipping and pastoral life of the parish. Corresponding to the order of the Prayer over the Oils in the episcopal rite (see pp. 288–9), it provides an introduction (following the Greeting), with the presentation and prayer of reception for the oil of the sick, the oil of baptism, and the oil of chrism. The president may speak briefly of the significance of each of the oils. The service then continues with the prayers of penitence. While the text says 'bishop' for each of the three prayers of reception, note that this is a mistake and will be corrected to 'president' in any future printings.

For further material on the significance of oil, see *Common Worship: Christian Initiation*, pp. 335–6 (the sign of the cross), 343, 345–8.

The Liturgy of Maundy Thursday

As with Palm Sunday, *Times and Seasons* provides a fully worked-out service, modelled on the earlier form in *Lent, Holy Week, Easter*. The rite is an Order 1 celebration of the Lord's Supper, with the optional addition of

- the ceremony of footwashing

- words at the Preparation of the Table, recalling the Passover

- the ceremony of the Stripping of the Sanctuary in the Conclusion

- provision for a 'watch'.

The Maundy Thursday liturgy is rich in themes, as illustrated by the readings:

- the washing of feet, part of the Gospel of the day (John 13.1-17)

- the *mandatum*, the new commandment, part of the Gospel of the day (John 13.31b-35)

- the institution of the Holy Communion (New Testament reading, 1 Corinthians 11.23-26)

- the Passover (Old Testament reading, Exodus 12.1-4, [5-10], 11-14).

It should be noted that this rite has a 'festal' feel to it, arising from the insight that the gift of the Holy Communion is a cause for joy and celebration, reflecting our gratitude for Christ's self-offering.

So the liturgical colour is white or gold and the Gloria in Excelsis is restored. As the rite proceeds, however, the atmosphere changes as the joyful 'Passover' feel of the Eucharist, with its themes of deliverance and salvation, gives way to thoughts of arrest, denial and desertion.

There are two introductory notes (p. 293). The first allows adaptation of the Words of Institution in the Eucharistic Prayer to 'in the same night that he was betrayed, that is, this very night'. The second refers to the custom of veiling the cross on the holy table and the processional cross in plain white linen. The veiling of crosses during Lent, or particularly in Passiontide, was once a popular custom in Anglican churches of a catholic tradition, following Roman practice. The reforms of Vatican II led to the demise of this tradition. While it did reflect the instinct to cover richly ornate ornaments as part of a growing austerity, it was also open to the criticism that at the very point in the liturgical year when the cross of Christ was most to the fore, the visual representations of that cross were hidden! In some churches, a more simple cross was substituted for this period.

It is worth thinking carefully about the setting of this service. Reflecting the Last Supper, it has a particular intimacy and depth. Is there a way in which this can be complemented by how the seating is arranged? For example,

- Can congregational seating be in the round, as if gathering around the Lord's table?

- Or is there space for the congregation to stand around the holy table for the Liturgy of the Sacrament?

- Or where the table is in the chancel, if the Liturgy of the Word is celebrated in the nave, is there room for the Liturgy of the Sacrament to be celebrated in the chancel?

The washing of feet   This is an optional part of the rite but has proved popular in many churches. It is often deeply meaningful for those who participate directly in it. There are a number of ways in which it can be done:

- the most representational way is for the president, imitating Christ, to wash the feet of 12 men, representing the apostles

- or, if this is felt to be too male dominated, twelve people, male and female, of different ages

- or, if 12 is deemed to be too many, a number of invited members of the congregation.

But this is not the only way.

> At All Saints, the worship committee, seeking to look creatively at how they celebrated Maundy Thursday, began with a Bible study of John 13.1-17. As they considered the text, the words of Jesus that seemed to stand out were, 'So, if I, your Lord and Teacher, have washed your feet, you also ought to wash one another's feet'. How could this be ritualized? In the end they came up with the following approach.
>
> It was made clear to the congregation in advance that all could participate, if desired, in the footwashing. Those wishing to do so were asked to come wearing suitable clothes (trousers and socks). Four jugs and basins with towels were provided at each of the four chairs on the platform in front of the nave altar. After the sermon, the president and assistant, wearing simple white albs, washed each other's feet. Members of the congregation then came forward to each of the four chairs. As one person sat down and removed their shoes, the next person washed their feet. Then the role was reversed. The result was that each person both had their feet washed and washed another's. The striking thing was the care and love with which this was done. Some were moved to tears, and for some the experience was one of reconciliation. As the footwashing took place, the choir sang the Taizé chant *Ubi caritas*. The order of service invited those not coming forward for footwashing to use the space to reflect on Christ's call to loving service in the readings and sermon.

Where this ceremony is used, it is worth purchasing suitable earthenware jug(s) and bowl(s), as well as towels.

Music can be used to good effect, especially versions of *Ubi caritas et amor*, the traditional anthem for the footwashing. James Quinn's metrical translation, 'God is love and where true love is', is particularly suitable (*Common Praise* 441, *New English Hymnal* 513), while churches with a choral tradition cannot do better than Maurice

Durufle's '*Ubi caritas*', Thomas Tallis's 'If ye love me', or S. S. Wesley's 'Wash me throughly from my wickedness'. Taizé chants, including more than one setting of '*Ubi caritas*', are also most effective.

The preparation of the table Here, the link with Passover is most clearly expressed in texts, first used in *Lent, Holy Week, Easter*, with clear allusions to the Jewish Passover liturgy (particularly the section 'Gamaliel's Constitution') and the ancient benedictions over the bread and the cup:

At the eucharist we are with our crucified and risen Lord.
We know that it was not only our ancestors,
but we who were redeemed
and brought forth from bondage to freedom,
from mourning to feasting.
We know that as he was with them in the upper room
so our Lord is here with us now.
**Until the kingdom of God comes
let us celebrate this feast.**

Blessed are you, Lord, God of the universe,
you bring forth bread from the earth.
Blessed be God for ever.

Blessed are you, Lord, God of the universe,
you create the fruit of the vine.
Blessed be God for ever.

The stripping of the sanctuary This tradition, long observed in 'catholic' parishes, has strong dramatic power in the transition from 'Last Supper' to contemplation of the arrest, desertion, denial and trial of Jesus. It is thus not merely utilitarian, as a way of preparing the church for Good Friday with the removal of hangings, but a symbol of Christ's desolation. Where it is done, it needs to be executed with care and reverence, and so a rehearsal is highly desirable. The holy table, having been cleared of all communion requisites, is stripped first by the president and an assistant. Other ministers may then assist in the removal of other items of furniture and liturgical and devotional objects. The stripping can effectively be done in silence, or Psalm 88 or verses from the Lamentations may be said or sung, either by the congregation or, better still, by one or two voices. Subdued lighting adds to the sense of drama and desolation. Again, where musical resources allow, Edward Bairstow's setting of the Lamentation cannot be bettered. The sense of Jesus' desertion can be further emphasized if the choir and ministers who entered in order then leave in disorder ('they all forsook him and fled').

The watch Some churches will wish to observe an extended watch, either for a specified period at the conclusion of the Eucharist, or until midnight, or even through the night until the Good Friday Liturgy. The spirituality here is identifying with the agony in the garden and all that follows it: 'Could you not watch with me one hour? Watch and pray, lest you enter into temptation.'

Times and Seasons gives provision for an extended series of Bible readings from the Farewell Discourses of St John's Gospel, with accompanying psalmody and much use of silence, concluding with the Gospel of the Watch (p. 304):

Year A   Luke 22.31-62
Year B   Matthew 26.30-end
Year C   Mark 14.26-end

The focus of the watch can be the now stripped holy table and sanctuary, with subdued lighting. Or, in some parishes, the focus will be the 'altar of repose', often decorated with flowers and greenery to symbolize the Garden of Gethsemane, as a place of reservation of consecrated eucharistic elements for the Liturgy of Good Friday (see below). Where this is done, a congregational procession follows the ministers, with the reserved elements, to the place of reservation, usually a side chapel or specially designated area of the church. Where there is a procession, it should perhaps be done simply, in marked contrast to the 'festal' processions used in some places on Corpus Christi. Alternatively, the president and the deacon (or an assistant minister) can take the reserved elements to the place of reservation, while the congregation remain in their places; the president and assistant then return to the sanctuary for the stripping, and finally everyone goes in procession to the altar of repose.

Where Bible readings are used, the place of reading should be chosen carefully, so that it does not obscure the focus of the watch. Alternatively, Bible readings and other suitable prayers and readings can be supplied for people to read privately as an aid to their devotions.

However, a silent watch is also most effective and, for some, further spoken words will be intrusive.

In some parishes, the Watch is accompanied by suitable quiet music, with short readings and prayers each half hour or hour. In other places, a series of optional activities is provided; for example,

- opportunities for creative writing
- painting and drawing
- prayer stations, focusing on aspects of intercession arising from the passion narratives
- writing letters or cards to prisoners of conscience
- provision of pictures of the passion to aid meditation.

Where the watch is not observed, *Times and Seasons* makes provision for a short dismissal rite, with brief gospel reading and effective form of dismissal (without response):

> Christ was obedient unto death. Go in his peace.

Here, of all occasions, the congregation should disperse in silence.

Agapes and Passover Seders

Lent, Holy Week, Easter included an outline for an *agape* within the context of Holy Communion. Some churches have valued the celebration of Holy Communion in the context of a meal, especially on Maundy Thursday. *Times and Seasons* declined to follow the earlier publication, partly because of scholarly uncertainty about the historical basis of something described as an *agape*, distinguishable from the Eucharist. For example, Paul Bradshaw in his book *Eucharistic Origins* (SPCK, 2004, pp. 29–30), commenting on the texts in the *Didache*, and drawing on an article by Andrew McGowan, writes thus:

> the whole concept of the *agape* is a very dubious one. It has served as a useful vague category in which to dump any evidence for meals that scholars did not want to treat as Eucharistic, regardless of whether the text itself described the meal as an *agape* or by some other title as here. What it is particularly vital to note is that

there is no evidence at all, except perhaps in the case of Tertullian, for early Christian communities that practised both a Eucharist and at the same time something else called an *agape*, but rather that where the latter use is used for a meal, it seems to be the name of the only form of Christian ritual meal existing in that community, the equivalent of what other Christian groups might call 'the Eucharist' or 'the Lord's Supper'. So, for example, Ignatius of Antioch appears to regard the words 'Eucharist' and '*agape*' as synonymous when he writes: 'Let that be considered a proper Eucharist, which is (administered) either by the bishop, or one whom he has entrusted (it) . . . It is not permitted without the bishop either to baptize or to hold an agape . . .' (*Smyrn.* 8).

This rather contradicts the introduction to 'The Agape within the Holy Communion' in *Lent, Holy Week, Easter*. However, where it is desired to hold a communion service in the context of a fuller meal, the agenda suggested in *Lent, Holy Week, Easter* is still legitimate; adapted to Order One, it would run:

The Gathering
Greeting
The introductory part of the meal
Prayers of Penitence
Collect

The Liturgy of the Word
Readings and Sermon
The main course of a simple meal may be taken here
Prayers of Intercession

The Liturgy of the Sacrament
The Peace
The second course may be taken here
Taking of the Bread and Wine
The Eucharistic Prayer
Giving of Communion
The consecrated bread and wine may be passed reverently round the tables or the communicants may move to a central point.

Prayer after Communion

Another increasingly common observance in Holy Week, especially on Maundy Thursday, is a Seder or Passover meal, sometimes also in conjunction with the Eucharist. Sensitivity needs to be shown in Christian adaptations of a Jewish observance, and good theological notes for Christian preachers and teachers are provided by the Council of Christians and Jews: see www.ccj.org.uk/documents/ EucharistandSeder. CCJ also publishes *The Seder*, by Clements and Montagu (CCJ, 2001).

Where such meals, eucharistic or non-eucharistic, are held in a church hall or meeting room, it is common for the congregation then to go into church for the Watch, thus marking the transition from Last Supper to Gethsemane.

Good Friday

Liturgical observance of Good Friday is a ready example of the diversity in the Church of England, partly related to churchmanship, but also to historical factors which over the years have led to the development of traditions concerning Good Friday. Some churches will hold more than one service, or there may be a range of services within a multi-parish benefice. There is also a widespread tradition of ecumenical services and walks of witness.

Lent, Holy Week, Easter provided an Anglican version of the traditional Roman/Western Liturgy of Good Friday. This has proved to be popular in many parishes and has undoubtedly contributed to a much greater degree of liturgical conformity on this most solemn day. However, many other approaches can be found, either in addition to or instead of the Liturgy:

- an all-age service
- the Way of the Cross
- Morning and/or Evening Prayer, or A Service of the Word
- Night Prayer
- the traditional three hours' devotion of readings, music and series of addresses
- a devotional service of readings, hymns and prayers

- all-age activities, such as the making of an Easter Garden, sometimes in parallel with worship in church
- a full celebration of Holy Communion
- an ecumenical march of witness, or specially devised ecumenical service
- musical devotions, such as Stainer's *Crucifixion* or Maunder's *Olivet to Calvary.*

Times and Seasons provides resources for many of these options in its Passiontide material, and the provision of a fully worked-out 'Liturgy of Good Friday' is not intended to limit creativity. *Together for a Season* provides eight all-age ideas for Good Friday worship, some of which draw on or amplify the *Times and Seasons* material, while the 'Head, hands and heart pathway' (pp. 112–15), and 'the Stations pathway' (pp. 116–19) provide additional approaches for all-age worship.

The Liturgy of Good Friday

The Liturgy has the following structure

The Gathering
The Collect

The Liturgy of the Word
Old Testament Reading
Psalm 22
New Testament Reading
The Passion Reading

The Proclamation of the Cross

The Prayers of Intercession

The Liturgy of the Sacrament
The Lord's Prayer
Giving of Communion
Prayer after Communion

The Conclusion
Prayer

It is worth remembering that the Liturgy of Good Friday continues a sequence of worship that began with the Maundy Thursday Eucharist.

Note 1 (p. 306) stresses the role of silence as being integral to the service; this complements the sense of prayerful meditation on the cross that is at the heart of Good Friday worship.

The Gathering The ministers enter in silence and a rubric suggests that all may kneel for a time of silent prayer. This indeed sets the tone of contemplation, and a focused corporate silence, especially when the congregation actually *does* kneel, can be a moving experience for all, particularly if it is given visual focus by the ministers kneeling or prostrating themselves, possibly at the chancel step. The president ends the silence by standing as the cue for the congregation to stand for the Collect.

The Liturgy of the Word The appointed readings are the same for all three years:

Isaiah 52.12–53.end
Psalm 22 (or 22.1-11 or 1-21)
Hebrews 10.16-25 or Hebrews 4.14-16; 5.7-9
John 18.1–19.42.

It is specified that silence is kept after each reading, even if a canticle or hymn is used, and that there should be silence between the Gospel and the sermon. The rite is deliberately austere, and for that reason note 1 also suggests that it is appropriate for the organ to be used only to accompany congregational singing.

The Gospel reading is by long tradition the Johannine passion, as also appointed in *The Book of Common Prayer*. Note 2 suggests that it may be read or sung by three or more people – see *Proclaiming the Passion*, pp. 34–41. The advice given for a dramatic reading on Palm Sunday applies equally here. Again, some churches present the passion narrative as a play or tableau, or use projected symbols or slides to illustrate the spoken word. It is customary to observe a short silence at the words 'Then he bowed his head and gave up his spirit', and in some places, it will be appropriate for the ministers and congregation to kneel at this point, before rising as the narrative continues. As in the rest of Holy Week, no Gospel responses are used. A sermon, however brief, is desirable on this day.

The Proclamation of the Cross The rubric (p. 309) states that the

Proclamation of the Cross may occur before or after the prayers of intercession. A good case can be made for both positions:

- in the earlier position, the Proclamation of the Cross follows directly on from the Liturgy of the Word and so is organically related to it;

- by following the Proclamation, the prayers become as it were the voice of Christ, interceding for the world he is redeeming.

However, if the order is reversed,

- the Proclamation of the Cross can take its place as the devotional climax of the rite, especially when there is no communion.

The rubrics state that a wooden cross may be brought into the church and placed in the sight of the people. So a visual symbol is not mandatory, although some churches might wish to project one or more images of the cross as an alternative. But surely there should be *some* visual focus, otherwise this aspect of the rite becomes very cerebral. A substantial, specially made wooden cross is to be preferred, with a base so that it can be positioned in a suitable place at the head of the nave or in the chancel. A drape in passion red material can add to the sense of engagement:

> His dying crimson, like a robe,
> spreads o'er his body on the tree:
> then am I dead to all the globe,
> and all the globe is dead to me.
> *Isaac Watts*

Again, the rubrics suggest that as the cross is carried in, the procession may stop three times for a responsory:

The cross of Christ.
**The cross on which the Saviour of the world was
    hung.**

(or)

This is the wood of the cross,
on which hung the Saviour of the world.
Come, let us worship.

This may be said or sung, and it is intended that musical settings for all the new *Times and Seasons* material will be forthcoming over the next few years. A sung setting is particularly desirable when the hymn 'Faithful cross' ('*Crux Fidelis*', *New English Hymnal* 517) is used (for another version, see *Common Praise* 115, 'O cross of Christ, immortal tree'). Where this hymn is used for the procession of the cross through the church, it can effectively be used as follows:

Two verses of the hymn (perhaps one sung by a soloist or choir and the other by the congregation). The procession stops.

Reponsory

Two more verses, the procession continuing. It then stops:

Responsory

Two more verses, the procession continuing. It then stops:

Responsory

Final two verses: the cross is placed in position.

The rubrics then make reference to 'appropriate devotions', while anthems are sung. This can be as simple as the congregation kneeling to sing 'When I survey', or members of the congregation coming forward to kneel for a few seconds before the cross, or to touch it or kiss it. For some, this will invoke fears of a piety, 'creeping to the cross', that the Reformation was careful to banish; however, then the concern was superstition, and while this must always be guarded against, it is miles away from the simple love and devotion to Christ which is displayed in churches today. Such a ceremony will never be mandatory, and, to quote the Prayer Book again, will be governed 'as each man's [sic] devotion best serveth'.

Times and Seasons provides four anthems: the first is the Reproaches, for which two versions are given. Both have been carefully written to minimize any anti-Semitism (to which the Introduction to the Season makes reference on page 259). The second version, from the Anglican Church of Canada, does not include any narrative from Israel's history (unlike the first). Anthem 2 draws on material from the Book of Revelation, Anthem 3 from 1 Timothy 3.16, and Anthem 4 from Psalm 67. Again, it is intended that musical resources will be forthcoming. However, there is a wealth of appropriate material from the hymn tradition and from contemporary worship songs that can appropriately be used at this point in the rite. Examples include:

- When I survey the wondrous cross

- O sacred head, surrounded

- Ah, holy Jesus, how hast thou offended?

- O dearest Lord, thy sacred head

- Jesu, grant me this I pray

- Were you there when they crucified my Lord?

- Come and see, come and see the King of love

- He was pierced for our transgressions

- It's your blood that cleanses me

- The cross has said it all

- What kind of love is this that gave itself for me?

The Prayers of Intercession These are also drawn from Canada, but reflect the ancient Roman form of intercession, with the structure:

- bidding

- silence

- response

- collect

The rubrics envisage that the president says the collects, with another minister leading the biddings. The scope of the intercessions is broad and spiritually demanding, befitting the sense of costliness of the day. When they follow the Proclamation of the Cross, the sheer visibility of the cross adds to the sense of joining with Christ in pleading for the world on the basis of his self-sacrifice.

The Liturgy of the Sacrament Unlike *Lent, Holy Week, Easter*, the rubrics do not make reference to a full celebration of communion, but clearly envisage a reception from elements previously consecrated on Maundy Thursday. This on its own, of course, does not rule out a full celebration, and it is perfectly possible to use the material of the Liturgy of Good Friday up to this point for this purpose. Nor does it assume that communion will be distributed at all; the opening rubric begins, 'If communion is to be distributed . . .'. The issue needs to be agreed locally. For example, some Christians will regard Good Friday as a 'fasting day' from reception of communion even if the communion is celebrated or distributed; some will be comfortable about receiving twice from a single consecration and some will not. Some will find that receiving communion is their complete response to Christ's self-giving, while others will regard it as detracting from their contemplation of the visible cross. Certainly for many, coming forward to venerate the cross is a kind of equivalent to coming forward to receive the sacrament.

The Conclusion The Conclusion is very brief; a single prayer, for which two options are given (the first from Eric Milner-White's *Procession of Passion Prayers* and the second adapted from *Lent, Holy Week, Easter*), with no further addition.

A rubric suggests that St John's account of the Burial of Christ may be read (John 19.38-42), and the wooden cross carried out; if this is followed, the earlier Passion Gospel ends at John 19.37. The Burial Gospel could effectively be read from the font, a symbol of Christ's tomb.

A Devotional Service

Where a simple devotional service of music and readings is required, perhaps as part of a 'three-hour devotion' in addition to 'The Liturgy of Good Friday', then reading through one of the passion narratives not read on either Palm Sunday or Good Friday in a given year can be effective. For example, using the Lukan material, the following form could be used:

> Response (*used after each reading*):
> God forbid that we should glory
> **save in the Cross of Christ our Lord.**

	At the entry of the ministers, all kneel for silent prayer
President	O crucified Jesus,
	Son of the Father,
	conceived by the Holy Spirit,
	born of the Virgin Mary,
	eternal Word of God,
All	**we worship you.**

O crucified Jesus,
holy temple of God,
dwelling place of the Most High,
gate of heaven,
burning flame of love,
we worship you.

O crucified Jesus,
sanctuary of peace and love,
full of kindness,
source of all faithfulness,
we worship you.

O crucified Jesus,
ruler of every heart,
in you are all the treasures of wisdom and knowledge,
in you dwells all the fullness of the Godhead,
we worship you.

Jesus, Lamb of God,
have mercy on us.

Jesus, bearer of our sins,
have mercy on us.

Jesus, redeemer of the world,
grant us peace.   *Presbyterian Church (USA)*

The Collect of Good Friday

Hymn or song
Reading 1   Luke 22.47-65   The betrayal and denials
Silence

Hymn or song
Reading 2   Luke 22.66–23.12   The trial before Herod
Silence

Hymn or song
Reading 3   Luke 23.13-31   The trial before Pilate
Silence

Hymn or song
Reading 4   Luke 23.32-49   The crucifixion
Silence

Brief intercessions
The Lord's Prayer

Hymn or song
Address

Hymn or song (with procession to the font)
Reading 5   Luke 23.50-56.   The burial
Song, such as 'Were you there when they crucified my
Lord?'
Collect of Easter Eve
Blessing

The number of readings may, of course, be varied according to the
shape of the service; the following readings, or some of them, could be
used from St Mark.

Reading 1	Mark 14.1-11	The priests' plot and the anointing
Reading 2	Mark 14.12-31	The Last Supper
Reading 3	Mark 14.32-52	The betrayal and arrest
Reading 4	Mark 14.53-72	The trial before the High Priest and Peter's denial
Reading 5	Mark 15.1-20	The trial before Pilate
Reading 6	Mark 15.21-39	The crucifixion
Reading 7	Mark 15.40-47	The burial

Another approach would be to centre on the narrative of the
crucifixion, supplemented by readings from the Epistles on the
meaning of the cross, for example:

Romans 3.21-26
1 Corinthians 1.18-25
2 Corinthians 5.14-21
Galatians 6.11-end
Colossians 1.18-23

Easter Eve (Holy Saturday)

Easter Eve is an a-liturgical day. In practice, most churches will be
occupied in making practical arrangements for Easter Day. By long
tradition, the communion is not celebrated. However, the set readings

for the Liturgy of the Word (at ante-communion) and Morning and Evening Prayer explore rich biblical themes, whereas in the Christian East the great theme of the harrowing of hell is to the fore. Where the offices are celebrated publicly, saying them near the font can assist the sense of watching at Christ's tomb. In some churches there is a tradition of Evening or Night Prayer for Easter Eve with preparation for Easter Communion. A. E. Housman's fine poem is resonant (sung to '*Unde et memores*'):

> If in that Syrian garden, ages slain,
> You sleep, and know not you are dead in vain,
> Nor ev'n in dreams behold how dark and bright
> Ascends in smoke and fire by day and night
> The hate you tried to quench and could but fan,
> Sleep well and see no morning, Son of Man.
>
> But if, the grave rent and the stone rolled by,
> At the right hand of majesty on high
> You sit, and sitting so remember yet
> Your tears, your agony and bloody sweat,
> Your cross and passion and the life you gave,
> Bow hither out of heav'n and see and save.

Ian Wallis has written a thoughtful book, *Holy Saturday Faith: Rediscovering the legacy of Jesus* (SPCK, 2000), which includes a liturgical rite exploring themes of loss, watching and waiting.

4 The Easter Liturgy

Rejoice, heavenly powers! Sing choirs of angels!
O Universe, dance around God's throne!
Jesus Christ, our King, is risen!
Sound the victorious trumpet of salvation!
Exsultet (The Easter Song of Praise),
Times and Seasons, p. 410

As it was in the beginning

Time was when what *Times and Seasons* calls 'The Easter Liturgy' had barely entered Anglican consciousness. Parishes of a catholic hue, in the wake of the Oxford Movement, may have observed an Easter Vigil, often on Easter Eve, but Easter Sunday morning was the heart of Easter Day worship for the vast majority of Anglicans, and in many places still is! However, the influence of *Lent, Holy Week, Easter: Services and Prayers* has led to the development of the Easter Liturgy as a significant celebration in many places, on Easter Eve as darkness falls, or early on Easter morning as dawn breaks, or as part of regular Easter morning worship. *Times and Seasons*, recognizing the 'mixed economy' in Anglican practice, has therefore included a raft of possibilities under the general heading 'The Easter Liturgy', including

- The Easter Liturgy: Pattern A and Pattern B

- The Dawn Service

- A Mid-Morning Eucharist on Easter Day using Elements from the Easter Liturgy

- An Outline Service of the Word for Easter Day

The result is that the Easter Liturgy provision in *Times and Seasons* runs to 102 pages! But before anyone loses the will to live, these services draw on a common core of material, bringing a distinctive character to the principal celebration on Easter Day, which is, after all, 'the feast of feasts'.

Historically, the Easter Vigil is one of the oldest forms of liturgy known to the Church. As the Introduction states (p. 323):

> From earliest times Christians have gathered through the night of Easter to recall the story of God's saving work, from creation through to the death and resurrection of our Lord Jesus Christ.

This is further amplified in the notes on Patterns A and B (pp. 324–5), and in the exposition of the four main elements of the Easter Liturgy on pages 326–7, namely

- The Vigil, a night-time service of readings and meditations on the story of salvation;

- The Service of Light, with the lighting of the Easter Candle, and the proclamation of the *Exsultet*, the Easter song of praise and triumph;

- The Liturgy of Initiation, with, where appropriate, Baptism and/or Confirmation, and the congregational Re-affirmation of Baptismal Vows;

- The Eucharist, the first Communion of Easter, as we are sacramentally reunited with Christ.

What shall we do?

Churches wishing to develop their celebration of Easter by drawing on the rich *Times and Seasons* provision need to consider what approach they are going to adopt. The aim has been to provide choice and flexibility rather than 'one size fits all'. Sometimes, there are many churches or places of worship within a single benefice, where a range of Easter services will be required at different times of day. Some will prefer to join in the large and grand celebrations that are now customary in cathedrals and greater churches. Here resources, especially music, are evident, and the bishop may be leading a diocesan or area confirmation as part of the Liturgy of Initiation. Some will have inherited a tradition of ecumenical worship, especially the popular 'dawn services' that enable a shared and atmospheric celebration of the resurrection before dispersing to denominational groupings for mid-morning worship.

Where a church decides to celebrate the Easter Liturgy, further questions need to be addressed:

- *Times and Seasons* provides two different patterns, A and B. What is the rationale for each pattern? Which pattern shall we adopt?

- When will the service be held? On Easter Eve, and if so, at what time? And for how long? Is the vigil element to be extensive, or curtailed? Could an all-night vigil be contemplated, and if so, how should it be planned and organized? On Easter Day, and if so, at what time? In the early morning, say 5am, or later, or as part of the usual mid-morning service?

- Is there to be any celebration of Christian initiation, as well as the renewal of baptismal vows?

- If the service is held on Saturday evening, will it include the Eucharist?

- Is there any way in which the Easter Liturgy can include children?

- Where there is more than one church building in a benefice, could a joint celebration be held? If so, when, and how can the joint celebration relate to other services in the benefice? Or could there be a united deanery celebration, or ecumenical celebration?

- What resources do we need? And what music? And how will the church be decorated?

Making choices

Page 327 sets out some of the possible answers:

- celebrating the Easter Liturgy as one service throughout the night, beginning on the evening of Holy Saturday and reaching its climax at dawn on Easter Sunday morning;

- holding the Vigil and Service of Light on Saturday evening, and leaving the baptismal and eucharistic liturgies for Sunday morning;

- gathering on Saturday evening or before dawn on Sunday for a short vigil, and leaving the rest of the Easter Liturgy to be celebrated later in the day;

- keeping the Easter ceremonies for the main service on Easter Sunday and omitting the Vigil altogether;

- relocating the worship to another significant place in or around the community.

Before looking at the possibilities in some detail, it will be helpful to set out a summary of the *Times and Seasons* provision.

The Easter Liturgy: Pattern A

See pages 324, 331–47, 367–71. This has the following basic structure:

- The Service of Light

- The Vigil of readings

- The Liturgy of Initiation

- The Liturgy of the Eucharist

- The Dismissal

The thinking behind this pattern is set out on page 324. The service begins with the lighting of the Easter Candle, followed by the Easter proclamation, the *Exsultet*, acclaiming the resurrection light of Christ. In his risen light, the following Vigil embraces

- a series of readings from the Old Testament

- the Easter Acclamation: Alleluia. Christ is risen.

He is risen indeed.

Alleluia, alleluia, alleluia.

- Gloria in Excelsis

- the Collect

- New Testament Reading (Romans 6.3-11)

- [Psalm 114]

- the Gospel of the Resurrection

- sermon

Here the Vigil is essentially used as 'an extended Liturgy of the Word'

(p. 324). The Liturgy of Initiation follows, with provision for baptism and confirmation where desired and Re-Affirmation of Baptismal Vows. The Easter Eucharist concludes the celebration.

The notes on pages 331–3 give helpful guidance on aspects of the ordering, choreography and symbolism of the rite.

The Easter Liturgy Pattern B

See pages 324–5, 351–71. This adopts a different structure:

- The Vigil

- The Service of Light

- The Liturgy of Initiation

- The Liturgy of the Eucharist

- The Dismissal

This pattern, with the Vigil of readings coming first, is described as 'a storytelling approach'. For more background read pages 324 and 325, where the notes recommend that the Vigil should be held, where possible, at night in a place separate from the church. It begins with a series of Old Testament readings, exploring the great themes of creation, exodus, sin and rebellion, God's faithfulness, and the hope of salvation. As a sense of anticipation grows during the vigil, the congregation moves to a place near the main entrance of the church where the Easter Candle is lit, leading the congregation into the church building. If candidates are being presented for baptism and/or confirmation, the Decision may take place during the Service of Light before the Easter proclamation (*Exsultet*). So in this pattern it is the Service of Light that embraces:

- the Easter Acclamation: Alleluia. Christ is risen.

He is risen indeed. Alleluia.

- Gloria in Excelsis

- the Collect

- New Testament Reading (Romans 6.3-11)

- [Psalm 114]

- the Gospel of the Resurrection

- sermon

Here, the Gospel of the Resurrection is the climax of the 'storytelling'; all finds its fulfilment in the dying and rising of Jesus.

As with Pattern A, a full set of notes (pp. 351–3) gives full guidance on the performance of the rite. In particular, note 2 stresses that any lighting needed for the Vigil of readings must not be confused with the new fire lit later on for the Service of Light. The introductory material on p. 325 includes the following important advice on the Vigil (see also note 2, p. 372):

> Pattern B lends itself to an adventurous approach. For example, the Bible readings could be dramatized or enacted, and each reading could be followed by silence, interactive Bible study, artistic activity (including the marking of the Easter Candle), discussion, testimony, drama, intercession, singing or whatever is appropriate for the setting. Choruses, spiritual songs or appropriate hymnody could replace the Psalm. If the Vigil is to last all night there could be specific points for eating and drinking that are related to the readings, until the climax is reached in the Service of Light and the Easter Eucharist.

The Vigil

See pages 372–97. While the Vigil is integral to Patterns A and B, *Times and Seasons* helpfully collates the Vigil resources separately, not least because there is significant choice in this element of the rite. The notes (pp. 372–4) recapitulate and expand on notes and rubrics elsewhere, covering

- the setting (especially in relation to Pattern B)
- a variety of styles
- lighting (related to Pattern B)
- the prayers and responses
- the choice of readings

Various patterns of readings are suggested. Note 5 states that a minimum of three Old Testament readings should be used, two of which are required, although both readings could be shortened according to need. The mandatory readings are:

- Genesis 1

- Exodus 14

Five sets of themed readings are then given:

- Baptismal theme

- Women in salvation

- Salvation theme

- Renewal theme

- Freedom theme

followed by a full list of 22 possible readings. Other schemes may be devised locally.

For the 22 readings, a full set of material is provided (pp. 376–97) including

- the reading

- psalmody

- psalm response

- silence

- with Pattern A: a versicle and response and christologically related prayer

- with Pattern B: a bidding with *berakah* prayer related to the theme of the reading.

The Dawn Service

See pages 325, 398–400. As the shape of this type of service is dictated by many local factors, the notes and rubrics allow for variation. Note 1 recognizes that a Pattern B-type vigil may precede it, while note 3 sets out a variety of possible contexts:

- a place of significance for the local community

- a hilltop

- a place of local religious significance

- near a cave (representing the empty tomb)

- a graveyard

- a garden

Note 5 suggests that the four elements of the Easter Liturgy should be considered, however 'informally and with a light touch': a Service of Light, the Vigil, the Liturgy of Initiation, and the Eucharist, and this is reflected in the Outline Shape on page 400, following Pattern B.

A Mid-Morning Eucharist on Easter Day using Elements from the Easter Liturgy

See pages 401–3. This makes provision for some of the Easter Liturgy ceremonies to be used at a mid-morning service in places where the Easter Liturgy as such is not celebrated. Note 2 includes the advice, 'It is important to present a mid-morning service in such a way that it does not seem to be a night service that is accidentally being celebrated during the day.' So, for example, where the *Exsultet* is used, the options 'This is the day', 'Crowning glory of all feasts' are used. It does allow for a *distinctive* beginning for what will be the principal Easter service in many churches, in the same way that the Commemoration of the Lord's Entry into Jerusalem is distinctive for Palm Sunday. So the main lights are switched off, the ministers go to the main entrance and the following structure is given:

- [acclamation]

- [marking of Easter candle]

- words of introduction

- lighting of Easter Candle

- procession of Candle [with lighting of congregational candles]

- [Exsultet]

- Easter acclamation

- Gloria in Excelsis etc

- [Re-affirmation of baptismal vows or Thanksgiving for the Resurrection]

A helpful 'all-age' approach to this service is set out in *Together for a Season* (pp. 145–53).

An Outline Service of the Word for Easter Day

See pages 404–7 and the last paragraph of page 327. Many churches attract very large all-age congregations on Easter Day and for reasons of accommodation may have more than one 'principal' service. This provision adapts the Easter ceremonies for a non-eucharistic context, using the same material as the mid-morning Eucharist above with the addition of concluding material (p. 407).

Instructions for Marking the Easter Candle

See pages 408–9. This gives diagrams and instructions for the prayers 'Christ, yesterday and today' and 'By his holy and glorious wounds' from the Service of Light. For the former, while in most places the president will simply trace the cross, Alpha and Omega, and the year with his thumb (often corresponding to the wax relief or transfer already on the candle), it is possible to cut the symbolic references using a suitable stylus or a nail.

The Exsultet

See pages 410–17. Various forms of this Easter Song of Praise are given:

- Form 1 also appears in the main text of Patterns A and B. Two alternative forms, the second metrical, are given for the Introduction ('Rejoice, heavenly powers!' or 'Sing, choirs of heaven!'). Optional responses are suggested for the main text, with the variant 'This is the night [day]', 'Most blessed of all nights [Crowning glory of all feasts]', according to circumstances. An alternative ending with explanatory note restores the reference to the work of bees, from the pre-Vatican II western tradition:

> Therefore, heavenly Father, in this our Easter joy
> accept our sacrifice of praise, your Church's solemn offering,
> this wax, the work of bees and the hands of your ministers.
> **[Glory to you for ever.]**
>
> As we gaze upon the splendour of this flame
> fed by melting wax conceived by mother bee,
> grant that this Easter Candle may make our darkness light.

For Christ the morning star has risen in glory;
Christ is risen from the dead and his flame of love still
    burns within us!
Christ sheds his peaceful light on all the world!
Christ lives and reigns for ever and ever!
Amen.

Exsultet, Times and Seasons p. 412

Musical settings for this new form of the *Exsultet* are beginning to appear, including the use of the traditional tone. This can be downloaded from the RSCM web site at http://www.rscm.com/info_resources/ exsultet.php

- Form 2 is a responsive form, with the evocative refrain 'all God's people sing and dance'

- Form 3 is a metrical version for tunes with 10.10.10.10. (e.g. Woodlands)

- Form 4 is a modern recasting of the *Exsultet* by Gregory Jenks, in a different register and employing bold imagery.

Welcoming the Easter Candle into the Church, with Prayers at the Easter Garden

See pages 418–20. This adaptation of the Service of Light is intended for use when the Easter Candle has been lit at an earlier service or at a service in another church. It has three main contexts:

- situations where there has already been a celebration of the Easter Liturgy on Easter Eve or very early on Easter Day but where the rank and file of the congregation were not present (i.e. the mid-morning Easter Day service);

- situations in multi-church or parish benefices where the Easter Liturgy was a united service, and where individual Easter Candles were lit from the 'host candle';

- situations where representatives of a local church attended the cathedral Vigil or a Vigil at a greater church (perhaps where the bishop was confirming) and where the candle was lit from the 'host candle'.

The Prayers at the Easter Garden may be used separately; they include a form of blessing and there are suggestions for actions which would be particularly suitable where there are children present.

Thanksgiving for the Resurrection

See pages 421–4. The form designated sections 1–4 was first published in *Lent, Holy Week, Easter*. The opening notes suggest a variety of uses:

- as an introduction to the Eucharist in Eastertide

  - Greeting
  - Sections 1, 2, (3), 4
  - Gloria in Excelsis

- as a processional at Evening Prayer

- section 2, as a processional to the font.

Alternatively, 'Thanksgiving for the Holy Ones of God' (*Times and Seasons*, pp. 558–60), with the response 'Alleluia, alleluia, alleluia', may be used, or the Easter Anthems (p. 424).

Pattern A or Pattern B?

From this mass of material, it may be helpful to set out some possible uses to assist churches to find a form that will help their ministry, mission and circumstances. The following illustrations show the rich variety of possible uses and contexts.

Pattern A

At St Peter's, there had been an Easter Vigil on Easter Eve for many years, but it was poorly attended. The vicar came to the conclusion that one reason for lack of support was that the service had never really been explained to the congregation. So during Lent she wrote articles for the magazine, explained the Holy Week liturgies in a Sunday sermon series, promised them one of the most beautiful services of the year and asked for support. Lifts were arranged for elderly members of the congregation. After consultation with the PCC, it was agreed that the service would begin at 8pm and last for 50 minutes. They would have the Service of Light, a short Vigil of readings, and renewal of baptismal vows. The Eucharist would be held over for Easter Morning.

The congregation responded and assembled in the darkened church. Everyone was asked to keep silence and there was a very focused and prayerful atmosphere. The Easter Candle was lit from a small fire near the main door. The prayers were amplified so everyone could hear. The Easter Candle was then carried in procession into church by a member of the choir, who acted as the 'deacon' and sang the *Exsultet* beautifully. Gradually the congregational candles were lit, filling the church with light. Four readings were chosen for the vigil, each followed by a short responsorial psalm sung by a cantor with simple congregational refrain, then silence and a collect. Then everyone stood for the Gospel reading. The vicar made the Easter Acclamation, 'Alleluia, Christ is risen', first quietly, then in a louder voice, and then shouted with joy, the congregation responding each time and with increasing volume 'He is risen indeed. Alleluia'. The lights were brought up, the organ played a dramatic fanfare, and the congregation broke into 'Ye choirs of new Jerusalem'. The vicar gave a short address, and as the hymn 'The strife is o'er' was sung, there was a procession to the font. There followed a joyful renewal of baptismal vows, the hymn 'Jesus lives', a final prayer and blessing. On leaving the church everyone was given a small Easter egg. Yes, people agreed, it was one of the most beautiful services of the year. They looked forward to returning in the morning to make their Easter Communion.

At St John's, there was a long tradition of holding the Easter Vigil as the first and principal Easter celebration on Easter Eve. No effort was spared in making it a splendid occasion, with a 'three-line whip' on attendance! The service began at 8pm in the churchyard round a bonfire. A careful rehearsal earlier in the day ensured that the large team of servers (including a thurifer), assistant ministers, readers, candidates for baptism (and in some years, when a bishop was present, confirmation) were well prepared. The Easter Candle was lit and carried into the dark church; as 'The Light of Christ' was proclaimed by the deacon, congregational candles were lit. Following the advice in note 13 (p. 332), the candidates for baptism, on entering the church, gathered and remained at the font. The *Exsultet* was proclaimed and then, by candlelight, a Vigil of seven readings, with responsorial psalms, silence and collects, was kept. The Easter Acclamation was then made and the congregation broke into a riot of noise as whistles, hooters and cheering greeted the resurrection, giving way to the joyful strains of the Gloria from the organ, which had been silent during the *Triduum*. The church bells were also rung at this point. The church candles on the altar and lectern were lit and the main lights switched on. The church had been lovingly and beautifully decorated. The Liturgy of the Word then continued, followed by a procession to the font using a sung version of section 2 of Thanksgiving for the Resurrection (*Times and Seasons*, p. 422). The Liturgy of Initiation was particularly joyful. Each baptism was greeted by the singing of the 'Celtic Alleluia', preceding the prayer of reception ('May God who has received you by baptism . . .'). At the congregational re-affirmation of baptismal faith, the vicar, using a large rosemary branch, joyfully sprinkled the congregation with the baptismal water. At the sharing of the Peace, the words 'The Lord is risen/He is risen indeed' were used. The baptismal candidates were then brought to seats of honour at the front of the nave and the Easter Eucharist was celebrated. After the blessing, the baptismal candidates were given their elegant baptismal candles and went in procession out of the church, as the bells greeted the end of the liturgy. The congregation lost count of how many times 'alleluia' was said or sung. The sense of faith and joy was tangible. After the service, fireworks and a party ensured a night to remember.

At St Andrew's, the new rector introduced the idea of the Easter Liturgy to the PCC's worship committee. Some members of the church had long wanted to hold a service to greet the dawn on Easter Day, and the committee warmed to the idea of a 5am celebration, even if some wondered whether anyone would turn up!

It was clear from discussion that the church youth group wanted to take part, and the Rector had the idea of asking the Scout Group to take care of the bonfire by having a sleepover in the Scout hut. Some members of the congregation volunteered to make a splendid full-works breakfast to follow the service. During Lent, people interested in attending signed up, and it was soon clear that there would be an all-age congregation of at least 80, including children and young people. Meanwhile, the organist and music group agreed to come, and a small group sat down to plan the service. It was agreed that it should last for about an hour and that Pattern A should form the basis of the service.

The time-table was:

4.30am The Scouts assemble the bonfire in the churchyard and light it

4.50am The congregation gathers around the bonfire

5.00am The service begins with the lighting of the Easter Candle

6.00am The service concludes

6.15am The breakfast begins with bucks fizz, followed by a full English

7.15am Egg rolling in the church car-park

The service was as follows:

Service of Light
Lighting of the Easter Candle

Procession into church with lighting of congregational candles

The Easter proclamation (*Exsultet*)

The Vigil
Five short readings were selected, followed by songs led by the music group, with percussion instruments for the children

Reading: Genesis 1.1-4a   God said 'Let there be light'
Song: 'O Lord our God, how majestic is your name'

Reading:	Genesis 22.1,2,6-13	The near sacrifice of Isaac
Song:	'Hallelujah, my Father'	
Reading	Exodus 14.21,22	The passing through the Red Sea
Song:	'How great is our God'	
Reading:	Ezekiel 36.25-28	I shall pour clean water upon you
Song:	'As the deer pants for the water'	
Reading	Ezekiel 37.1, 4, 11-14	Breathe on these dead; let them live
Song:	'For I'm building a people of power'	

The Easter acclamation (repeated three times and greeted by much noise)

Song: 'He has risen, Jesus is alive'

Collect

New Testament Reading: Romans 6.3-11

'Celtic Alleluia'

The Gospel of the Resurrection, dramatized by the youth group

Hymn: 'Alleluia! Alleluia! Give thanks to the risen Lord', during which the congregation went in procession to the font

Renewal of Baptismal Vows

As the music group led the songs 'River wash over me' and 'I am a new creation', the congregation all went to the baptismal water to wash themselves.

The Easter Eucharist

The Peace

Procession to the chancel: 'Love's redeeming work is done'

The Communion

Final hymn: 'The day of resurrection'.

Everyone was delighted with the service, and it was clear that a new parish tradition had been established. Also, the vast majority of the congregation was hungry for more, and so looked forward to returning to church for the 10.30am service!

Together for a Season provides an all-age Saturday evening service based on Pattern A (see pp. 125–31, 138–44).

Pattern B

At St Francis, the tradition had developed on Maundy Thursday of holding a 'Seder Eucharist' in the church hall, followed by a 'Gethsemane meditation' in church with the stripping of the sanctuary. A similar pattern was adopted for the Easter Vigil. At 7.30pm on Easter Eve, the congregation gathered in the church hall. They wanted to create a 'camp-fire' feel and were able to borrow a very effective artificial 'bonfire' from the church Scout Group as the focus for the Vigil. Six readings were selected, followed by short meditations on each of the readings prepared by members of the congregation, silence, and a suitable song to finish. During the silences, members of the congregation could contribute a thought, comment or short prayer. The Vigil lasted for an hour. Then the congregation went from the hall and gathered by the main door of the church. A fire had been lit in a brazier, and the service continued with the Service of Light and the Easter Eucharist.

By adopting the pattern of beginning in the hall and then going into the church building twice over, the unity of the services of the *Triduum* was emphasized and the Passover themes were underlined. In particular, the words of the *Exsultet* resonated with the Seder Eucharist, and during the service in church, the use of the Easter Anthems ('Christ our Passover is sacrificed for us') further strengthened the connection.

At Holy Cross the congregation greatly valued a very reflective approach to Holy Week. Each evening, apart from Maundy Thursday, but including Good Friday, Compline preceded by an address was said in the spacious chancel. For Easter Eve, it was decided to hold a Vigil of readings.

The introduction from page 354 was used, including the lighting of the lectern candles, followed by 'Lighten our darkness'. Six readings followed, including Genesis 1.1–2.4a and Exodus 14.10-end; 15.1a. After each reading, silence was kept, concluded by the collect. After the sixth reading, the narrative of the death and burial of Jesus from St John's Gospel was read (John 15.31-42). After a silence, the vicar led a prayer of preparation for Easter Communion and the Lord's Prayer and concluded with the Collect for Easter Eve. The congregation dispersed in silence.

On Easter Sunday, the Parish Eucharist began with the Service of Light, and included the renewal of baptismal vows.

The future of Christ Church had been uncertain for many years because of a dwindling congregation. However, it had good plant and a central position. The deanery Pastoral Committee decided to reconstitute it as a 'youth church' and appointed a Pioneer Minister to build up a congregation of young people. This met with some success, and when the oversight group sat down to think about celebrating Easter, it was the idea of an all-night service that caught the imagination. Pattern B seemed just the job, and so plans were made for an extended overnight vigil, beginning at 8pm and culminating in a dawn Eucharist. The chancel of the church became a 'Vigil zone'; and the nave a place for a variety of planned activities throughout the night. The Vigil began with the introduction from *Times and Seasons*, p. 354. Each hour, everyone would gather in the chancel; the lights were switched off, leaving two candles illuminating the lectern, and there would be a ten-minute reflection point, using

- a vigil reading

- a Taizé chant

- a time for open prayer

Throughout the night workshops were held, including music, creative writing, drama, art, and an excellent presentation by the Pioneer Minister on 'the passion in film'. From 4.30am, the church was prepared for the concluding worship. The unlit Easter Candle was already in position in the 'Vigil zone'. At 5am, the minister led a meditation on watching and waiting. At 5.30am, the Easter Candle was lit and a version of the 'all God's people shout and sing' *Exsultet* was sung to a setting written by one of the group.

> The Gospel was read, the minister announced the Easter
> Acclamation, and an extended period of praise and worship
> followed. The group then went to the west end font to renew their
> baptismal vows, and then to the middle of the nave, where the
> holy table was situated, just as light began to stream through the
> east window. After a joyful Eucharist 'in the round', an Easter
> breakfast of fish and bread (John 21.9-14) concluded the
> celebration.

Together for a Season provides another model for an all-night service
with sleepover (see pp. 131–44).

Symbols which speak

It is worth giving consideration to some of the basic symbols of the rite.

The Easter (Paschal) Candle The Easter Candle is the pre-eminent
symbol of the presence of the risen Christ, the Light of the world. It
should therefore be a large and impressive candle, the best a church can
obtain or afford. Many church suppliers now produce candles with
beautifully designed and crafted wax reliefs, far more impressive than
transfers. It should be placed on a suitable stand, situated in a
prominent place in the church, and lit at all principal celebrations from
Easter Day to Pentecost. Many Easter candle-stands include provision
for integrated flower arrangements, which enhance the dignity of the
candle.

Congregational candles If the Vigil of readings follows the lighting of
the Easter Candle and therefore is likely to take some time, many
church suppliers now offer 'vigil candles', 12″ × 3/8″, with suitable
drip-shields.

Initiation candles Where there are candidates for baptism and/or
confirmation, their candles should be distinguishable from the
congregational candles, say 10″ or 12″ × 7/8″.

Lectern The lectern for the Vigil readings should be dignified and
carefully appointed because it symbolizes the visible means of grace,
'Christ in all the Scriptures' (Luke 24.44-47).

Baptismal water Whether or not baptism and/or confirmation are
administered, the Easter Liturgy includes re-affirmation of baptismal
vows. This can be accompanied by sprinkling or, where possible,

members of the congregation can approach the font to make the sign of the cross with water or apply water to themselves. The font itself is a symbol of Christ's tomb.

Noise, music and light See note 10, page 332. The Easter Acclamation, 'Alleluia! Christ is risen', can be wonderfully greeted by a cacophony of noise from percussion instruments, bells, hooters, football rattles, pots and pans, and whistles, as well as crashing chords from the organ or a brass fanfare. The switching on of all lights in a previously candle-lit church also powerfully symbolizes the dawning of resurrection light upon the world. The first use of the Easter Acclamation is also enhanced by repetition of alleluias, as in the *Times and Seasons* text (see p. 338, Pattern A; p. 361, Pattern B):

> Alleluia. Christ is risen.
> **He is risen indeed. Alleluia, alleluia, alleluia.**

Or, repetition of the whole acclamation, with crescendo:

First, said quietly:	Alleluia! Christ is risen. **He is risen indeed. Alleluia!**
Second, said louder:	Alleluia! Christ is risen. **He is risen indeed. Alleluia!**
Third, in a loud voice:	Alleluia! Christ is risen. **He is risen indeed. Alleluia!**

The Easter Acclamation may, of course, be used at a number of points during Easter Day worship (preceding the final blessing is particularly appropriate) and as an acclamation during Eastertide.

Flowers and decorations Easter lilies are a long established sign of resurrection and symbol of Christian hope, but all spring flowers add to the sense of new life after the rigours and austerity of Lent. Suitable banners can also add to the sense of celebration. The Easter Garden is an important symbol of the story of Easter in many churches, and a potential means of involving people of all ages in its construction.

Easter clothes While the liturgical colour is white or gold, the old tradition of 'Easter clothes' is worth restoring, so that the congregation gathers in festal mood. Candidates for baptism and confirmation should be encouraged to think creatively about what they will wear. For some, changing into 'Easter clothes' after baptism and confirmation will be an important symbol of their new life in Christ.

In short, the words of the Introduction are apposite: 'All the resources of the church – music, flowers, bells, colours – are used to celebrate Christ's resurrection' (p. 323).

Music The RSCM produces (annually), as part of its *Sunday by Sunday* planner, a list of suggested music for congregation, choir and organ to support the Easter Liturgy. This includes hymns and songs which relate to the Principal Service Lectionary vigil readings.

5 Easter

This joyful Eastertide,
away with sin and sorrow.
My Love, the Crucified,
has sprung to life this morrow:
had Christ, that once was slain,
n'er burst his three day prison,
our faith had been in vain:
but now hath Christ arisen.

G. R. Woodward

Party on

I was once asked to lead Evensong on Low Sunday and I was invited to choose the hymns. When I presented my four choices from *Hymns Ancient and Modern*, all from the Easter section, the organist retorted, 'Wasn't it Easter last week?' Rather like Christmas, the common view in society at large is that Easter is a long weekend from Good Friday to Easter Monday. For the Church, however, Easter is a season, beginning on Easter Sunday and extending for fifty days until the great Feast of Pentecost (Whitsunday). Of course, recovery of the idea of *fifty* days is a rather recent re-evaluation of Eastertide. Older generations had become accustomed to the idea of 'the Great Forty Days' from Easter Day to Ascension Day (Acts 1.3), followed by Ascensiontide, and leading into Whitsuntide. So, for example, in the Calendar of *The Book of Common Prayer* the sequence is:

- Easter Day
- the six days of Easter week
- five Sundays *after* Easter
- The Ascension Day
- Sunday after Ascension Day

- Whitsunday

- the six days of Whitsun Week

So, in effect, there are three 'seasons' here: Eastertide, Ascensiontide, and Whitsuntide.

Common Worship has followed the reform of the Calendar in the Roman Catholic Church after Vatican II by restoring the older tradition of a single season of 50 days, as stated in the Introduction to the Season (p. 427). This views the interval between the resurrection and the giving of the Spirit as a *single* unit, on the understanding that the resurrection of Jesus is intrinsically linked to the outpouring of the Holy Spirit upon the Church. This is illustrated by the Post Communion prayer appointed for the Day of Pentecost:

Faithful God,
who fulfilled the promises of Easter
by sending us your Holy Spirit
and opening to every race and nation
the way of life eternal:
open our lips by your Spirit,
that every tongue may tell of your glory;
through Jesus Christ our Lord.

So the *Common Worship* Calendar sets out this season as follows:

Easter

Easter Day
Monday to Saturday of Easter Week
The Second Sunday of Easter
The Third Sunday of Easter
The Fourth Sunday of Easter
The Fifth Sunday of Easter
The Sixth Sunday of Easter

Ascension Day
From Friday after Ascension Day
    begin the nine days of prayer before Pentecost
The Seventh Sunday of Easter – *Sunday after Ascension Day*

Pentecost (Whit Sunday)

Here, it can immediately be seen that the Sundays are designated Sundays *of* Easter rather than Sundays *after* Easter; the period from Ascension Day to the Eve of Pentecost is still Eastertide, and thus Eastertide *concludes* with the Day of Pentecost.

'Alleluia' is the great cry of the season, reflected in the great Easter hymns, but also in the liturgy. As well as the Seasonal Provisions in the *Main Volume* (pp. 316–17), Order One Holy Communion includes an acclamation following the Greeting (see also note 5, p. 330):

Alleluia. Christ is risen.
He is risen indeed. Alleluia.

an invitation to communion:

Alleluia. Christ our Passover is sacrificed for us.
Therefore let us keep the feast. Alleluia.

and a distinctive form of dismissal:

Go in the peace of Christ. Alleluia, alleluia.
Thanks be to God. Alleluia, alleluia.

for use throughout the season.

Leaders of worship should be aware that in Order One at the Gathering there are a number of distinctive elements.

The Trinitarian formula,

In the name of the Father
and of the Son,
and of the Holy Spirit.
Amen.

is an invocation. The next element,

The Lord be with you
and also with you.

is a greeting. The following text from Easter Day to Pentecost,

> Alleluia. Christ is risen.
> **He is risen indeed. Alleluia.**

is an acclamation.

Only the Trinitarian formula is optional. In *ASB* Rite A, the acclamation was an *alternative* to the greeting. Order One corrects this, distinguishing carefully between the presidential greeting and the complementary seasonal acclamation.

Times and Seasons provides five blocks of material for Eastertide:

- Seasonal material (pp. 428–42)

- Stations of the Resurrection (pp. 443–68)

- The Liturgy of Ascension Day (pp. 469–81)

- Seasonal Material for use from Ascension to Pentecost (pp. 483–9)

- The Liturgy of the Feast of Pentecost (pp. 491–502).

This can be supplemented by material in *New Patterns for Worship*, especially the Resource Sections under the headings 'Resurrection', 'Ascension' and 'Holy Spirit' and the Seasonal Service of the Word: Christ is Risen: a Service for Easter (pp. 402–6). All-age resources may be found in *Together for a Season: All-age seasonal resources for Lent, Holy Week and Easter* (pp. 196, 197–227).

Seasonal material

The Easter Garden An opening rubric (p. 428) suggests that during the season, prayers of penitence might appropriately be led from the Easter Garden. This, for example, might form part of an opening procession, with the order

- The Greeting from the west end (or back) of the church

- All or first part of the processional hymn

- Prayers of penitence at the Easter Garden

- Second part of the processional hymn and/or Gloria in Excelsis

- The Collect

Invitations to Confession Three texts are given, the first, from 1 Corinthians 5, from the Seasonal Provisions in the *Main Volume*. The second, drawing on Romans 6 baptismal imagery, and the third, also from Romans 6, are from David Silk's book *In Penitence and Faith*.

Kyrie Confessions Two forms are provided; the first, adapted from the *Roman Missal*, appeared in *Enriching*; the second is a new text, drawing creatively on the disciples' experience in the Easter Gospel narratives:

> Like Mary at the empty tomb,
> we fail to grasp the wonder of your presence.
> Lord, have mercy.
> **Lord, have mercy.**
>
> Like the disciples behind locked doors,
> we are afraid to be seen as your followers.
> Christ, have mercy.
> **Christ, have mercy.**
>
> Like Thomas in the upper room,
> we are slow to believe.
> Lord, have mercy.
> **Lord, have mercy.**

Confession This responsive confession, adapted from *Church Family Worship*, is from the *Main Volume* 'Authorized Forms of Confession' section (*Main Volume*, p. 125).

Act of Penitence This distinctive Eastertide addition to the Seasonal Provision is intended for the main Sunday Eucharist in Eastertide. It provides an alternative penitential rite as part of the Gathering. The form is:

> *The president prays over a vessel of water*
>
> God our Father,
> your gift of water brings life and freshness to the earth;
> in baptism it is a sign of the washing away of our sins
> and the gift of life eternal.

Sanctify this water, we pray.
Renew the living spring of your life within us,
that we may be free from sin
and filled with your saving health;
through Christ our Lord.
Amen.

The president and people are sprinkled.
Meanwhile suitable hymns, songs or anthems may be sung.

The president concludes with this or another authorized absolution

May the God of love and power
forgive you and free you from your sins,
heal and strengthen you by his Spirit,
and raise you to new life in Christ our Lord.
Amen.

This ceremony consciously recalls the renewal of baptismal vows at the Easter Liturgy, and makes explicit the link between baptism and forgiveness as stated in the Nicene Creed: 'We acknowledge one baptism for the forgiveness of sins.' It helpfully links Easter Day and the Day of Pentecost as primary baptismal occasions, and reminds the congregation of the call to walk in newness of life because we have died and been raised with Christ (Romans 6.1-4; Colossians 3.1-12). Where this use of water is unfamiliar, it should be made clear to the congregation that this is a *penitential* rite; members of the congregation should be calling to mind their sins while the sprinkling is taking place, as the necessary condition for receiving absolution.

This form is adapted from the Rite of Blessing and Sprinkling Holy Water from the *Roman Missal*; the absolution is adapted from the *Scottish Liturgy 1982* (Scottish Episcopal Church). As part of the Gathering, it is most appropriately celebrated between the Greeting and the Gloria in Excelsis. It can be done in a number of ways. One possibility would be for the congregation to gather around the font for the Gathering rites and then to go in procession during the singing of the Gloria to the place where the Liturgy of the Word is celebrated. If the font is used, water consecrated at the Easter Liturgy could be used throughout Eastertide. In this case, the prayer 'God our Father . . .' would be omitted, but another could be substituted, such as the prayer from Thanksgiving for Baptism from *Common Worship: Daily Prayer* (p. 306):

> Blessed are you, sovereign God of all,
> to you be glory and praise for ever.
> You are our light and our salvation.
> From the deep waters of death
> you have raised your Son to life in triumph.
> Grant that all who have been born anew by water and
>   the Spirit
> may daily be renewed in your image,
> walk by the light of faith,
> and serve you in newness of life;
> through your anointed Son, Jesus Christ,
> to whom with you and the Holy Spirit
> we lift our voices of praise.
> Blessed be God, Father, Son and Holy Spirit.
> **Blessed be God for ever.**

Alternatively, and especially if the font is not located in a congenial place, a bowl of water could be placed on a convenient table and then carried by an assistant minister as the president sprinkles the people.

Gospel Acclamations Five forms are given; the fourth is from the *Main Volume* Seasonal Provision. Forms 1 and 3 are 'I am' sayings (Bread of life and Resurrection and the Life), form 2 is from John 6, and form 5 is a responsive 'Alleluia':

> Jesus Christ is risen from the dead.
> **Alleluia.**
> He has defeated the powers of death.
> **Alleluia.**
> He has the words of eternal life.
> **Alleluia.**

Intercessions Three forms are provided: the first two, suitable for Easter Day to Easter 6, are drawn from *Enriching*, the latter based on the 'I am' sayings. The third form, also from *Enriching*, recalls the ascension and so is suitable for the period from Ascension Day to the Eve of Pentecost.

Introductions to the Peace Three forms are provided, the first from the

Main Volume, the second, recalling the Easter Anthems, based on 1
Corinthians 15.20, and the third drawn from the Emmaus story.

Prayers at the Preparation of the Table Of the four prayers, the first
and fourth are from the Canadian *Book of Alternative Services*; the
second, based on the Emmaus story, is from Aotearoa-New Zealand's
A New Zealand Prayer Book; and the third, the 'Be present' prayer, is
from the *Main Volume*.

Prefaces Four short prefaces are given, all found in *Enriching*; the first
is from the *BCP/Main Volume*, the second and third from the *President's
Edition* (having been in *ASB*), and the fourth from the *Roman Missal*.

Extended Prefaces Of the two forms given, the first is from the *Main
Volume*, adapted from Alan Griffith's translation from the Ambrosian
Rite; the second is drawn from the 'Thanksgiving' section of *New
Patterns* (p. 250), based on 1 Corinthians 15:

We give you thanks and praise
for the gospel we have received.
Christ died for our sins. Alleluia.
He is risen indeed. Alleluia.

Death comes to us all through Adam,
and sin reigns for a time.
New life without end comes through Christ,
and he reigns for ever. Alleluia.
He is risen indeed. Alleluia.

Death, where is your victory?
Death, where is your sting?
Death is swallowed up in victory,
the victory he gives us in Christ Jesus. Alleluia.
He is risen indeed. Alleluia.

We have been crucified with Christ,
and live his risen life,
to praise you for ever with angels and archangels.
Holy, holy, holy Lord . . .

This is one of a series of texts in *New Patterns* where biblical passages
are recast as responsive thanksgivings, some of which are suitable as
extended prefaces. While it is clear that this is essentially a prayer to

God, it includes rhetorical 'direct address' to the congregation and, after 1 Corinthians 15, to death itself. Another example, based on the accounts of Jesus' coming to his disciples in the resurrection appearances, is given in *New Patterns* on page 250 (G77). This illustrates the possibility of writing 'home-grown' prefaces for Eucharistic Prayers A, B and E, particularly when A Service of the Word is combined with a celebration of Holy Communion. *New Patterns* sets out the ground rules on page 222, including the directive,

---

- If the Preface is specially composed, the president says,

  'And now we give you thanks . . .'

  and then offers brief thanksgivings in the form of 'We thank you that . . .' or similar words. They normally include thanksgiving for

  - creation
  - redemption
  - the continuing work of the Spirit.

- They should not conclude with 'Amen'. The president concludes by saying

  'Therefore with angels and archangels . . .' (Prayers A, B and C)

  (or)

  'And so we gladly thank you, with saints and angels . . .' (Prayer E)

  Eucharistic Prayers D, G and H are not suitable for this approach.

Blessings The four Easter blessings of *ASB* Rite A are reproduced (one text is mistakenly given twice: P3 and P5!); the additional text (P6) is from New Zealand, emphasizing the word 'new':

May Christ,
who out of defeat brings new hope and a new future,
fill you with his new life;
and the blessing . . .

An Alternative Dismissal for Easter In common with many *Times and Seasons* texts, this extended dismissal emphasizes the spirituality of

> Send us out in the power of your Spirit
> to live and work to your praise and glory.

It gives the structure:

- Acclamation, from Canada's *Book of Alternative Services* and included in *Enriching* and *New Patterns*

- Dismissal Gospel: John 11.25, 26

- Extended blessing, from *Enriching*

- Dismissal: a catena of texts, adapting the Order One dismissal texts with alleluias.

Acclamations The acclamation from the Alternative Dismissal is reproduced, along with a form based on 2 Timothy 2 from *New Patterns*.

Short Passages of Scripture Eight passages are given; the first four are particularly suitable as part of the Gathering or the introduction to A Service of the Word; the last four could be used at the Preparation of the Table, in the Post Communion, or at the conclusion of a non-eucharistic service.

Further extensive resources for Eastertide can be found in *Together for a Season* (pp. 171–227); see also *New Patterns* in the 'Resurrection' resources section, and in the sample service, 'Christ is risen: A Service of the Word in Easter' (pp. 402–6).

The Stations of the Resurrection

As the Introduction states (p. 443), Stations of the Resurrection are a relatively modern complement to Stations of the Cross. Like the latter, the beauty of this form of devotion is that it can be adapted easily, used by congregations of varying sizes, and undertaken simply or as the basis of an elaborate Easter processional. The Introduction stresses the nature of the resurrection appearances as personal encounters with the risen Christ; therefore silence and space are essential as we seek a fresh encounter with Christ today.

The Notes (p. 444) give helpful guidance, including the use of images (note 1), movement (note 2), and use with Holy Communion (note 6). The Gathering and the Conclusion are mandatory and nineteen 'stations' are provided, although it seems highly improbable that all nineteen would be used in one act of worship; rather, a suitable number may be selected, or, as note 3 suggests, a few could be used each week throughout Eastertide.

Each station has an identical pattern:

• versicle and response

• reading

• reflection or meditation

• prayer

• acclamation

Note 5 states that hymns or songs, music and drama may be added at suitable points. Some of the 'narrative' Easter hymns, such as 'Ye sons and daughters of the King' (*New English Hymnal* 125), 'O sons and daughters, let us sing' (*Common Praise* 154) or 'Light's glittering morn bedecks the sky' (*Common Praise* 149), or 'Good Joseph had a garden' (*Common Praise* 146), can be effective, a verse or two sung at each station.

The stations are

I	The earthquake
II	Mary Magdalene finds the empty tomb
III	The disciples run to the empty tomb
IV	The angels appear to the women
V	Jesus meets the women
VI	The road to Emmaus
VII	Jesus appears to the disciples
VIII	Jesus promises the Spirit
IX	Jesus commissions the disciples
X	Jesus breathes the Spirit in the upper room
XI	Jesus reveals himself to Thomas
XII	Jesus appears at the lakeside
XIII	Jesus confronts Peter
XIV	Jesus and the beloved disciple
XV	Jesus appears to over five hundred at once

> XVI   Jesus commissions the disciples on the mountain
> XVII The ascension
> XVIII Pentecost
> XIX   Jesus appears to Saul (Paul)

Out of this, various 'tracks' could be chosen, for example,

- a Johannine track: stations II, III, VII, IX, X, XI, XII, XIII, XIV

- a Luke-Acts track: stations IV, VI, VII, VIII, XVII, XVIII, XIX

- a 'personal encounter' track: stations IV, VI, XI, XIII, XIV, XIX

Or other tracks could be devised, using the resurrection narratives. An all-age adaptation of the stations may be found in *Together for a Season* (pp. 228–38).

A visual focus for the stations is helpful. Note 1 refers to the fact that publications on the stations are beginning to appear, and directs people to the World Wide Web. It also suggests that images could be created locally, perhaps at an Easter workshop. Some churches have used posters or distributed packs of postcards of great works of art. But there are other possibilities. For example, using the church building can be effective:

- the font, as a symbol of the empty tomb: stations I–III

- the Easter Garden, as a symbol of Jesus' encounter with the women: stations IV and V

- the holy table, for the walk to Emmaus: station VI

- the Easter Candle, as a symbol of Jesus' presence with his disciples: stations VII–XI

- a large cross, symbolizing Thomas' bereavement and inability to believe: station XI

- perhaps a stained-glass window, representing an aspect of the resurrection or portraying Peter or John: stations III, XIII, XIV

- the chancel (east end), as a symbol of the ascension and giving of the Spirit: stations XVII–XIX.

Or selected stations may be illustrated by flower arrangements. This does not demand a full-blown 'flower festival' (although that is one possibility), but some Flower Guilds may value the opportunity to give creative expression to aspects of the Easter story through arrangements. Or, as note 5 suggests, the stories can be mimed or dramatized.

At St Mark's, the idea of 'Stations of the Resurrection' caught the imagination of the youth group, who were responsible for a monthly evening service. They selected six stations, and over a number of weeks prepared resources for the service:

- one group painted large posters, portraying each station

- one group wrote some short reflections on each story

- one group prepared prayers

- one group thought about music; a number of them played musical instruments: guitars, flute, violin.

The service was very informal; the group decided to use the church hall for the service; posters were hung at different points in the hall; around each station there were a few chairs and some scattered cushions. As the instruments were portable, the music group moved from station to station. At each station there was

- a responsory

- a reading

- a song

- a meditation

- a prayer

- the song 'He is Lord'

They ordered the service as follows:

The Gathering

Times and Seasons pages 446–7, including Charles Wesley's hymn 'Christ the Lord is risen today', sung to Easter Hymn.

Station 1: Mary Magdalene finds the empty tomb; including Graham Kendrick's 'Led like a lamb to the slaughter'.

Station 2: The Road to Emmaus; including Marty Haugen's 'On the journey to Emmaus'.

Station 3: Jesus and Thomas, including Rick Founds' 'Lord, I lift your name on high'.

Station 4: Jesus appears to more than 500 at once; including Noel and Tricia Richards' 'All heaven declares the glory of the risen Lord'.

Station 5: The ascension; including David Mansell's 'Jesus is Lord! Creation's voice proclaims it'.

Station 6: Pentecost; including Chris Bowater's 'Holy Spirit, we welcome you'.

The Conclusion

Times and Seasons, page 468; including Tim Hughes and Ben Cantelon's 'The greatest day in history'.

As an alternative to Stations, an Easter service of readings and music could easily be constructed, using the Gathering and Conclusion section of Stations of the Resurrection, a form of intercession, and one of the patterns of readings from the Eastertide section of *Enriching*:

Pattern 1   Isaiah 25.1-9
           Psalm 113

           Jeremiah 31.1-14
           Psalm 116.1-9

           Zephaniah 3.14-end
           Psalm 118.1-9

           Isaiah 42.11-16
           Psalm 118.14-18

           Zechariah 8.1-8
           Psalm 118.19-28

           Revelation 1.10-18
           Te Deum, part 2

           John 21.1-14

Pattern 2   Acts 5.17-32
           Psalm 2

Acts 10.34-43
Psalm 111

Acts 13.26-41
Psalm 16.7-end

Acts 17.16-31
Psalm 138

Acts 26.1-23
Psalm 117

1 Corinthians 15.3-11
The Easter Anthems

Luke 24.13-35

The Liturgy of Ascension Day

This great day of joy and triumph is sadly often neglected in the contemporary Church. However, Canon B 14 states that Holy Communion shall be celebrated in parish churches on all principal Feast Days, and Ascension Day, with its great hymns and joyful themes, is an excellent opportunity for creative liturgy, with a parish party to follow!

Times and Seasons provides a fully worked-out order for the Eucharist, with two distinctive additions for this day. An extended Gathering rite includes an Introduction and Ascension Reading (Acts 1.4-11). The Introduction, which may be in any suitable words, sets the scene for the liturgy:

Dear brothers and sisters in Christ, for forty days we have been celebrating with joyful hearts the resurrection of our Lord Jesus Christ, his bursting from the tomb and his defeat of the power of sin and death. He appeared to his disciples many times and told them about the kingdom of God.

Today we recall how he left this earth and returned to his Father, ascending into heaven to take his throne over all dominions and powers. Trusting in his reign over all creation, and submitting to his kingly yet loving rule, let us hear the story of his parting.

The Ascension Reading follows, concluded with the Easter
Acclamation, and words of invitation by a minister:

> Seeing we have a great high priest who has passed through the
> heaven, Jesus the Son of God, let us offer him the praise worthy
> of his name.

The Gloria in Excelsis follows, although a great Ascension hymn such
as 'Hail the day that sees him rise', or an extended time of praise would
also be appropriate. One very effective way of staging this, in church
buildings where there is sufficient space, is for the Gathering to be held
at the west end, followed by a joyful procession around the church to
the place of the Liturgy of the Word. The use of banners and flags can
add to the sense of celebration.

The second distinctive feature comes in the Dismissal. This makes
explicit the link between Ascension Day and the coming of the Spirit,
inaugurating the period of focused prayer for the Spirit's renewal, and
looking forward to the Day of Pentecost to come. The order is:

- (hymn)
- reading: Acts 1.12, 13a, 14
- silence
- responsory
- silence, or a reflective hymn
- the blessing
- the dismissal

The Acts reading commemorates the disciples returning to Jerusalem
and giving themselves to prayer. The following silence is thus
integral to a sense of expectant waiting. The responsory takes up
the theme:

> As we wait in silence,
> **make us ready for your coming Spirit.**
>
> As we listen to your word,
> **make us ready for your coming Spirit.**

As we worship you in majesty,
make us ready for your coming Spirit.

As we long for your refreshing,
make us ready for your coming Spirit.

As we long for your renewing,
make us ready for your coming Spirit.

As we long for your equipping,
make us ready for your coming Spirit.

As we long for your empowering,
make us ready for your coming Spirit.

Further silence or a reflective hymn or song may follow, such as a Taizé chant, or a hymn or song of invocation. The extended Trinitarian blessing takes up Ascension and Spirit themes; the short blessing is related to the Spirit

May the Spirit,
who set the Church on fire upon the day of Pentecost,
bring the world alive with the love of the risen Christ.
And the blessing . . .

while the dismissal emphasizes expectant waiting:

Waiting expectantly for the promised Holy Spirit,
go in the peace of Christ. Alleluia, alleluia.
Thanks be to God. Alleluia, alleluia.

In churches where, for pastoral reasons, the ascension is celebrated on the Seventh Sunday of Easter, the Liturgy of Ascension Day may also be used.

An all-age adaptation of the Liturgy of Ascension Day (eucharistic or non-eucharistic) may be found in *Together for a Season* (pp. 154–61). This includes making the sign of the cross in glitter mixed with oil, or by using 'glitter sticks', available from most stationers. It recalls both baptism and the 'ashing' ceremony of the beginning of Lent, but whereas the latter recalls our mortality, this celebrates our sharing in Christ's glory through his resurrection and ascension.

The words used as the sign of the cross is made, based on John 11.4, are

> I sign you with the cross, the sign of Christ.
> Proclaim God's glory, and may the Son of God be glorified
>   through you.

When accompanied by careful explanation, this can be extremely effective as well as fun!

Seasonal material from Ascension to Pentecost

Page 482 gives a useful introduction to Pentecost (from the Greek *pentekoste*, 'fiftieth'). The New Testament states that Jesus died at the Jewish Passover festival, and that the Spirit came on the Jewish Feast of Pentecost, fifty days after Passover. The Venerable Bede gives an excellent summary of the biblical background:

The Jewish feast of the Law is a foreshadowing of our feast today. When the children of Israel had been freed from slavery in Egypt by the offering of the paschal lamb, they journeyed through the desert toward the Promised Land, and they reached Mount Sinai. On the 50th day after the Passover, the Lord descended upon the mountain in fire, and with the sound of a trumpet and with thunder and lightning, he gave them the ten commandments of the Law. As a memorial . . . he decreed an annual feast on that day, an offering of the first-fruits, in the form of two loaves of bread, made from the first grain of the new harvest, which were to be brought to the altar . . . Just as the Law was given on the 50th day after the slaying of the lamb, when the Lord descended upon the mountain in fire; likewise on the 50th day after the resurrection of our Redeemer . . . the grace of the Holy Spirit, descending in the outward appearance of fire, was given to the disciples as they were assembled in the upper room.

The Introduction sets out the close link between Ascension and Pentecost, and so gives the background for the re-ordering of the Calendar. We are still in Eastertide, but the emphasis shifts to that of anticipating the coming of the Spirit and then celebrating the Spirit's presence as Eastertide comes to joyful conclusion on Pentecost itself.

Care will need to be taken in making choices from this bank of material. The ascension and Spirit themes overlap, but some material will make more sense for Ascension Day to Easter 7 (when perhaps the theme of ascension dominates), and other material for the week leading up to Pentecost, when the promise of the Spirit is more prominent. Some material, like the Extended Preface for the Day of Pentecost, belongs to that day only.

Invitations to Confession Four forms are given, the first from the *Main Volume* (p. 320), and the second and third from *Enriching*, all relating to the work of the Spirit; the fourth, unusually with non-inclusive language and based on the ascension text in Ephesians 4.8, is by Nicolas Stebbing CR.

Kyrie Confessions Of the two forms given, the first is from *Enriching* and recalls the work of the Spirit, and the second, also by Nicolas Stebbing, is on ascension themes.

Gospel Acclamations Both forms are from the *Main Volume* Seasonal Provisions (p. 320, and p. 318 respectively).

Intercession A single form, with thanksgiving and intercession based on the diverse graces and ministries of the Spirit, is from *Enriching*.

Introductions to the Peace Two forms are provided, the first adapted from 1 Corinthians 1.22 from the *Main Volume*, and the second, based on Galatians 5.22,23, from *ASB*.

Prayers at the Preparation of the Table The first prayer is adapted from *The Book of Alternative Services* of Canada, and the second from *A Prayer Book for Australia*.

Prefaces Form 1 is from the *Main Volume*, form 2 originally from *ASB*, and form 3 is a fine text from *Enriching*, adapted from Canada:

> And now we give you thanks
> because in fulfilment of your promise
> you pour your Spirit upon us,
> filling us with your gifts, leading us into all truth,
> and uniting peoples of many tongues
> in the confession of one faith.
> You give us power to proclaim your gospel to all nations
> and to serve you as a royal priesthood.

> Therefore we join our voices with angels and archangels,
> and with all those in whom the Spirit dwells,
> to proclaim the glory of your name,
> for ever praising you and saying
> **Holy, holy, holy Lord . . .**

Extended Preface The Ascension preface from the *Main Volume* (p. 321), although a rubric refers to the Pentecost Extended Preface, used on Whitsunday only (see *Main Volume*, p. 321).

Blessings The short forms are from the *Main Volume* and *Enriching*; the extended form is also from *Enriching*.

Acclamation An ascension text, drawing on Ephesians 1 and Colossians 3 from *Enriching*.

Short Passages of Scripture All the passages selected relate to the ascension.

In some places, the Eve of Pentecost will be the ideal occasion for celebrating Christian initiation or holding a vigil of prayer and readings. For the latter, patterns of readings are given in *Enriching*:

Pattern 1	The Coming Spirit
	Deuteronomy 34
	2 Samuel 2.1-4, 10; 1 Samuel 23.1
	2 Kings 2.1-15 *or* 9-15
	Isaiah 64.1-7
	Revelation 21.1-4, 10, 22-end; 22.1-5
	Ephesians 4.7-13
	John 17.1-11
Pattern 2	The Spirit in Acts
	Acts 3.1-16 *and/or* 4.5-12
	Acts 5.12-32 *or* 17-32
	Acts 8.5-8, 14-17
	Acts 10.34-end
	Acts 18.24–19.7
	1 Corinthians 2. 1-13
	John 15.26–16.7

The pattern of the service could be:

- The Blessing of Light: *Common Worship: Daily Prayer* (pp. 110–11), including the Pentecost Light Prayer (p. 284)

- The Pattern of Readings with music, concluding with the Gospel

- Intercession and the Lord's Prayer

- The Collect

- Blessing and dismissal

Celebrating initiation

Common Worship: Christian Initiation provides a number of resources for celebrating initiation at Pentecost. The material is set out as follows:

- Celebration of Baptism and Confirmation within a Vigil Service on the Eve of Pentecost (pp. 135–49) – a fully worked-out service

- Seasonal Provisions: Easter/Pentecost (pp. 156–60)

The Liturgy of the Feast of Pentecost

The Day of Pentecost is one of the great days of the liturgical year, celebrating the gift of the Spirit and the birth-day of the Church. Red is the liturgical colour, recalling the 'tongues as of fire' resting on the heads of the infant community. Flowers and other decorations should reflect this theme; if the congregation can be persuaded to come to church wearing red items of clothing, all the better. Local churches will decide their pattern of worship on this day according to custom and pastoral needs. Various questions will need to be asked:

- Is the principal service to be eucharistic?

- Is there an all-age element to the service?

- Will Christian initiation be celebrated?

- Will the Easter Candle be ritually extinguished, and if so, when?

- As the Early Church went out and proclaimed Christ, is there a public witness aspect to the worship?

The Times and Seasons service is intended as the Principal Service for the Day of Pentecost and it bears an organic relationship to the Liturgy of Ascension Day. Like the latter, it includes an extended Gathering and Dismissal. While the service is eucharistic in form, it can easily be adapted to become a Service of the Word.

The Gathering has the structure:

- the Greeting
- introduction
- responsory
- silence
- the Pentecost Reading
- prayer for personal renewal
- Gloria in Excelsis
- the Collect

This is intended to take up where the Ascension Day rite left off, with reflective and expectant prayer, commemorating the first disciples as they waited in the upper room. The Introduction acts as a reprise of the 50 days of Easter:

Jesus Christ, whom we worship, is our crucified, risen and
   ascended Lord
and we have walked with him through his journey of love.
We have faced the agony of his suffering and death on a cross.
We have rejoiced at his bursting free from the bonds of death.
We have enjoyed his risen presence with us
and his revelation of himself through the breaking of bread.
We have seen his return to the throne before which every knee
   shall bow
and every tongue confess that this Jesus is Lord.
And now, with the followers of his own time,
we await the coming of the promised Holy Spirit,
   his gift to his people,
through whom we make Christ known to the world.

This is followed by a responsory, echoing that of Ascension Day:

> As we wait in silence,
> **fill us with your Spirit.**
>
> As we listen to your word,
> **fill us with your Spirit.**
>
> As we worship you in majesty,
> **fill us with your Spirit.**
>
> As we long for your refreshing,
> **fill us with your Spirit.**
>
> As we long for your renewing,
> **fill us with your Spirit.**
>
> As we long for your equipping,
> **fill us with your Spirit.**
>
> As we long for your empowering,
> **fill us with your Spirit.**
>
> *Silence is kept.*

After the silence, the Pentecost Reading, Acts 2.1-11, then follows, concluded with the acclamation

> The Lord is here.
> **His Spirit is with us.**

An optional rite of Prayer for Personal Renewal follows, including optional anointing with the oil of chrism. A designated person presents oil to the president:

> Oil for the renewal of God's people.
>
> *The president says*
>
> Be with us, Spirit of God;
> **nothing can separate us from your love.**

> Breathe on us, breath of God;
> **fill us with your saving power.**
>
> Speak in us, wisdom of God;
> **bring strength, healing and peace.**

The rite provides a form for the blessing of the chrism; however, it is more appropriate if oil blessed by the bishop on Maundy Thursday is used. Personal ministry may then follow, during which suitable hymns and songs may be sung, concluded with an acclamation. The rite continues with the Gloria and the Collect.

At St Philip's Church it was usual for prayer ministry to be offered at the more informal evening service. The church worship group was excited by the provision in *Times and Seasons* for anointing on the Day of Pentecost. The church had started using the oil of chrism at baptisms for the prayer 'May God who has received you by baptism into his Church, pour upon you the riches of his grace . . .' They used the chrism lavishly, pouring it from a jug on to the heads of the candidates, and indeed, the church building was filled with the perfume. For the vicar, this spoke powerfully of the generous outpouring of the anointing Spirit, and demonstrated that God in Christ dignifies women and men as daughters and sons of God, who now share the aroma of Christ (2 Corinthians 2.14,15). It also became an important sign of empowerment for Christian ministry and discipleship. For the Day of Pentecost, the text from Isaiah 61 set the theme:

> The spirit of the Lord God is upon me,
> because the Lord has anointed me . . .

The anointing came after the Sermon, which had expounded Isaiah 61.1-3. The prayers on page 493 of *Times and Seasons* were used, but then members of the congregation were invited to go to one of five stations around the church building, each one based on a theme from the passage:

> The spirit of the Lord God is upon me,
> because the Lord has anointed me . . .

1. to bring good good news to the oppressed

2. to bind up the broken hearted

3. to proclaim release to the prisoners

4. to proclaim the year of the Lord's favour

5. to comfort all who mourn

At each station there were posters showing needs in the locality or aspects of the ministry of the church to which individuals wished to respond and receive the empowered love of the Spirit. For example, 'to proclaim the year of the Lord's favour' focused on the church's evangelistic ministry, while 'to comfort those who mourn' embraced both bereavement support but also a ministry of intercession for many people experiencing loss of differing kinds. At each station, prayer ministry was offered, along with anointing. The Taizé chant, '*Veni, Sancte Spiritus*', provided a prayerful and fitting background.

In the Liturgy of the Word, a rubric directs that where the Acts reading has been used earlier, only one reading precedes the Gospel:

Year A	Numbers 11. 24-30 *or*
	1 Corinthians 12.3b-13
Year B	Ezekiel 37.1-14 *or* Romans 8.22-27
Year C	Genesis 11.1-9 *or* Romans 8.14-17

The Dismissal has the following structure:

- Blessing of Light

- Commission

- Conclusion

After the Post Communion prayer(s), the ministers go to the Easter Candle. Where practicable, the congregation could gather around the Easter Candle. A benediction, adapted from Michael Vasey's Light Prayer for Pentecost in *Enriching*, is said:

Blessed are you, sovereign God, overflowing in love.
With Pentecost dawns the age of the Spirit.
Now the flame of heaven rests on every believer.
Strong and weak, women and men tell out your word;
the young receive visions, the old receive dreams.
With the new wine of the Spirit
they proclaim your reign of love.
Amid the birth pangs of the new creation
the way of light is made known.
Source of freedom, giver of life,
blessed are you, Father, Son and Holy Spirit.
Blessed be God for ever.

Congregational candles are lit and a hymn may be sung. The Commission, with its colourful word 'dare', challenges God's people to live and walk in the Spirit:

For fifty days we have celebrated the victory of our Lord Jesus Christ over the powers of sin and death. We have proclaimed God's mighty acts and we have prayed that the power that was at work when God raised Jesus from the dead might be at work in us.

As part of God's Church here in N, I call upon you to live out what you proclaim.

Empowered by the Holy Spirit, will you dare to walk into God's future,
trusting him to be your guide?
By the Spirit's power, we will.

Will you dare to embrace each other and grow together in love?
We will.

Will you dare to share your riches in common and minister to each other in need?
We will.

> Will you dare to pray for each other until your hearts beat with the longings of God?
> **We will.**
>
> Will you dare to carry the light of Christ into the world's dark places?
> **We will.**

If this is the final service of the day, the Easter Candle may be extinguished. The rite concludes with the repetition of the acclamation, 'The Lord is here/His Spirit is with us', and the president says

> Today we have remembered the coming of God's power on the disciples and we invite that same Spirit to drive us out into the wild places of the world.

The congregation then goes in procession out of the church, if weather permits, or to the back of the church for the blessing and dismissal.

An all-age Eucharist for the Day of Pentecost, adapted from *Times and Seasons*, may be found in *Together for a Season* (pp. 161–70).

6 Trinity to All Saints

> Through all the changing scenes of life,
>   in trouble and in joy,
> the praises of my God shall still
>   my heart and tongue employ.
> *Nahum Tate and Nicolas Brady,*
> *after Psalm 34*

Trinity to All Saints is not a season as such, although the *Common Worship* Calendar gives a sense of cohesion by following *The Book of Common Prayer* in designating Sundays in this period as Sundays after Trinity. In reality we are in so-called 'Ordinary Time', the long 'green' period stretching through the summer.

Of course, there are festivals and commemorations during this period, and *Times and Seasons* provides material for four of them in this section:

- Trinity Sunday

- The Day of Thanksgiving for the Institution of Holy Communion (Corpus Christi)

- Dedication Festival

- Bible Sunday

There are others; Lammas and Harvest Thanksgiving fall in this part of the year (see Chapter 7) and *Common Worship: Festivals* provides material for major festivals, including the Visit of the Blessed Virgin Mary to Elizabeth (31 May), the Birth of John the Baptist (24 June), the Transfiguration of Our Lord (6 August), the Blessed Virgin Mary (15 August), Holy Cross Day (14 September) and Michael and All Angels (29 September), as well as Apostles and Evangelists. For the four festivals and commemorations in this section of *Times and Seasons*, a bank of Seasonal Resources is provided which may be used at the

Eucharist or A Service of the Word. The Collects and Post Communion Prayers are also included for the first three.

Trinity Sunday

> Holy, holy, holy! Lord God almighty!
> early in the morning our song shall rise to thee;
> holy, holy, holy, merciful and mighty!
> God in three persons, blessed Trinity.
>
> *Reginald Heber*

With the great and joyful festival of the Day of Pentecost, the 'seasonal' part of the church year comes to its conclusion. The next day, Monday, we are back in 'Ordinary Time', the liturgical colour is green, the Easter Candle (where used) is put in its traditional place near the font, where it is lit for baptism (and confirmation). The Easter Candle is also used in many places at funerals, where it should stand in a prominent place near the coffin as a symbol of the risen presence of Christ.

However, on the Sunday after Pentecost, we return to festal celebration with Trinity Sunday, the great festival of the Godhead, coming logically on the first Sunday after the completion of 'seasonal time' with its incarnational cycle (Advent to Candlemas) and its Paschal cycle (Lent to Pentecost). For a note on the historical origins of Trinity Sunday, see the final paragraph of 'Introduction to Pentecost' (p. 482).

Seasonal Provisions for Trinity Sunday can be found in the *Main Volume*, pp. 322–3. The 'Creeds and Affirmations of Faith' section in *Main Volume* (pp. 138–48) also has useful material, see especially sections 1, 3, 6 and 7. For example, no. 7 runs:

Let us declare our faith in God.

We believe in God the Father,
from whom every family
in heaven and on earth is named.

We believe in God the Son,
who lives in our hearts through faith,
and fills us with his love.

> **We believe in God the Holy Spirit,**
> **who strengthens us**
> **with power from on high.**
>
> **We believe in one God;**
> **Father, Son and Holy Spirit.**
> **Amen.** *cf Ephesians 3*

Further resources may be found in *New Patterns for Worship*, in the Resource Sections under 'Father, Son, and Spirit'. To this, of course, is added the rich tradition of Trinitarian hymns and songs, both those in the 'Trinity Sunday' section of hymnbooks, and those that structurally reflect on the rich doctrine of God that we celebrate as Christians, such as:

- Affirm anew the threefold name (Timothy Dudley-Smith)

- Father of heaven, whose love profound (Edward Cooper)

- Father, in whom we live (Charles Wesley)

- Father, we adore you (Terrye Coelho)

- Father, we love you (Donna Adkins)

- Holy, holy, Lord God almighty (Jimmy Owens)

- I bind unto myself today (C. F. Alexander, after St Patrick)

- I, the Lord of sea and sky (Dan Schutte)

- Lead us, heavenly Father, lead us (James Edmeston)

- Thou, whose almighty word (John Marriott)

- We give immortal praise (Isaac Watts)

Credal hymns, such as David Mowbray's 'We believe in God Almighty', Timothy Dudley-Smith's 'We believe in God the Father' (see *Main Volume*, p. 146), or Graham Kendrick's 'We believe in God the Father', are also appropriate.

Seasonal provision for baptisms and confirmations celebrated on or near Trinity Sunday may be found in *Common Worship: Initiation Services* (pp. 150–5).

Times and Seasons resources

Invitations to Confession: Four forms are provided; the first is from the *Main Volume*, the second and third are from *Enriching*, and the fourth is a new text:

> We have too often exchanged the worship of the living God for
>   idols of our own imagining.
> As we gather to offer our praises to the holy and undivided
>   Trinity,
> and to worship him in spirit and in truth,
> let us call to mind our sins.

Kyrie Confessions Two forms are provided, both from *Enriching*; the latter draws on Isaiah 6, the Old Testament reading in Year B.

Gospel Acclamation From the *Main Volume*, it echoes the *Gloria Patri*, 'Glory to the Father, and to the Son, and to the Holy Spirit', and Revelation 1.8.

Intercession The text is from *Enriching*, based on Edward Cooper's hymn text, 'Father of heaven, whose love profound'.

Introduction to the Peace Also from the *Main Volume*, it originated in *Patterns for Worship*.

Prayer at the Preparation of the Table A new text based on the *Trisagion*:

> Holy God,
> holy and strong,
> holy and immortal,
> give us the bread of everlasting life,
> and make us branches of the true vine.

Prefaces The first, from *ASB*, is in the *Main Volume*; the second is a new text, skilfully alluding to 2 Corinthians 4.6 and 3.18:

> And now we give you thanks, most gracious God,
> holy and undivided Trinity:
> because you have given us the light of the knowledge of God

> in the face of Jesus Christ,
> that we may grow into your likeness,
> and be changed from glory to glory.

Extended Preface From the *Main Volume*, and drawing on the Prayer Book Proper Preface and Te Deum; it originated in *Enriching*.

Blessings and Ending The short blessing is from the *Main Volume*; two forms of extended blessing are given from *Enriching*, the first based on the Aaronic Blessing (Numbers 6.24-26), and the second based on a prayer of Bishop Thomas Ken. An ascription of praise (P4), also adapted from Thomas Ken, is likewise from *Enriching*.

Acclamations Of the two forms, the first, with verses from Revelation 4 and 5, is from *Enriching*, and the second, combining the song of the seraphs from Isaiah 6.3 and verses from Psalm 29, is a new composition.

Short Passages of Scripture Six passages are provided; the first one, from Isaiah 6, is particularly suitable for the Gathering; the others could be used at a Eucharist, at the Preparation of the Table, or in both eucharistic and non-eucharistic services at the conclusion.

Seasonal Provisions for Christian Initiation, embracing Epiphany/Baptism of Christ/Trinity, are included in *Common Worship: Christian Initiation* (pp. 150–5).

At Holy Trinity Church, Trinity Sunday was observed with a morning Sung Eucharist, using the enrichment material from *Times and Seasons*. For the evening service, using the provisions of A Service of the Word, the following pattern was adopted:

As the ministers enter, the president places a representation of the Rublev 'Old Testament Trinity' icon on a stand at the head of the nave; the congregation sing the Iona round:

> *Gloria, Gloria, Gloria*
> *in excelsis Deo*

President   The grace of our Lord Jesus Christ,
             and the love of God,

	and the fellowship of the Holy Spirit be with you all
All	**and also with you.**
Minister	One seraph called to another and said: 'Holy, holy, holy is the Lord of hosts; the whole earth is full of his glory. S1

Three members of the congregation carry forward a large round candle with three wicks and place it on a stand before the nave altar.

As the first wick is lit, one says:

> I will light a light
> in the name of the Maker
> who lit the world
> and breathed the breath of life for me.

As the second is lit, the second says:

> I will light a light
> in the name of the Son
> who saved the world
> and stretched out his hand to me.

As the third is lit, the third says

> I will light a light
> in the name of the Spirit
> who encompasses the world
> and blesses my soul with yearning.

All	**We will light three lights for the Trinity of love: God above us, God beside us, God beneath us: the beginning, the end, the everlasting One.** *Iona Community*
Hymn	'Hail, gladdening light'
Collect	for Trinity Sunday, said by the president
Reading	2nd Service Lectionary

Hymn	'O Trinity of blessed light'
Reading	2nd Service Lectionary
Canticle	

The three members of the congregation who lit the candle lead the Canticle 'Praise to God the Holy Trinity' (*Enriching*, pp. 75–6).

1.	Glory to the Holy and undivided Trinity;
2.	Father, Son and Holy Spirit
3.	three persons in one God
All	**Glory to God, Father, Son and Holy Spirit.**

1.	Perfectly one from before time began;
2.	one in being and one in glory;
3.	dwelling in love; three persons, one God.
All	**Glory to God, Father, Son and Holy Spirit.**

1.	Incarnate Son, in suffering forsaken;
2.	Father, giving and forgiving;
3.	Spirit, bond in joy and pain.
All	**Glory to God, Father, Son and Holy Spirit.**

1.	Eternal Father, the Fountain of Life;
2.	Risen Son, the Prince of Life;
3.	Spirit of freedom, Giver of Life.
All	**Glory to God, Father, Son and Holy Spirit.**

1.	Truth, Word and Power;
2.	Lover, Beloved and Friend;
3.	Hope without end; Joy beyond words.
All	**Glory to God, Father, Son and Holy Spirit.**

Sermon	
Hymn	'Lead us, heavenly Father, lead us'
The Prayers	

The prayers are led in the form of biddings around the themes of unity and diversity. The first section embraces thanksgiving for diversity in the life of the world, the church, and the local community. The second section embraces prayer for reconciliation within the world, the church, and the local community. Members of the congregation are invited to come forward, light a tea-light, and place it before the candle and icon, making a short response, 'I give thanks . . .' or 'I pray for . . .' The prayers conclude with the Lord's Prayer.

The Conclusion

The ministers and congregation move in procession around the church building singing St Patrick's Breastplate. All gather round the candle and the icon. After the hymn, a period of silence is kept.

Minister	Acclamation, *Times and Seasons*, p. 512, R2
President	Extended Blessing, *Times and Seasons*, p. 511, P2
Hymn	'May the grace of Christ our Saviour'
Minister	Go in peace. Rejoice in God, Father, Son and Holy Spirit.
All	**Thanks be to God.**

The Day of Thanksgiving for the Institution of Holy Communion (Corpus Christi)

Author of life divine
who hast a table spread,
furnished with mystic wine
and everlasting bread,
preserve the life thyself hast given,
and feed and train us up for heaven.
Charles Wesley

While Jesus' institution of the Holy Communion is universally commemorated on Maundy Thursday, that commemoration is set in the much broader context of his impending passion. Corpus Christi, as it is popularly called, provides the opportunity to give thanks for the gift of the Eucharist in its own right and was established in the western Church from the thirteenth century. Because it was associated with the doctrine of transubstantiation, it was suppressed in the Anglican Calendar at the Reformation. Its use was restored in some Anglican churches through the Oxford Movement, and the 1928 Prayer Book recast it, and thus broadened its appeal, as a day of thanksgiving for the institution of Holy Communion. Corpus Christi is traditionally celebrated on the Thursday following Trinity Sunday. Thursday makes an explicit link with the institution of the Eucharist on Maundy Thursday. This day of thanksgiving first appeared officially in the Church of England Calendar in *ASB 1980* as a commemoration. In *Common Worship* its observance is optional, and it may be kept either as a commemoration or as a festival (see p. 27 of *Times and Seasons* for further details). The contemporary Roman Catholic practice in England and Wales is to transfer Corpus Christi to the First Sunday after Trinity, but there is no provision for this in the *Common Worship* Calendar.

Times and Seasons resources

Times and Seasons provides its usual bank of resources; while these do not demand a Eucharist, the nature of this day dictates that they would most naturally be used to supplement Order One. Much of the material is derived from the 'Eucharist' section of *Enriching*, including

- A1, the Invitation to Confession based on the *BCP* text 'Ye that do truly . . .'

- B1 and B2, the Kyrie Confessions, the first based on Psalm 43, and the second adapted from the *Roman Missal*

- H1, the Intercession

- J1 and J2, Introductions to the Peace, the first from *ASB*/Order One, and the second based on Matthew 5.23, 24

- L1–4, the short Prefaces

- P1 and P2, the short and extended Blessings

- P3, the 'Ending' text, 'Wisdom has set her table . . .'

- R1, the Acclamation, based on John 6

The distinctive *Times and Seasons* contributions to this section are the Prayer at the Preparation of the Table, a newly written text:

God our sustainer,
receive the gifts we bring before you,
and feed us continually with that bread which satisfies
    all hunger,
your Son our Saviour Jesus Christ.

and the Extended Preface, adapted from the *Roman Missal*:

It is indeed right and good,
our duty and our salvation
always and everywhere to give you thanks and praise
holy Father, almighty and eternal God,
through Jesus Christ our great high priest.
He offered himself to you as the Lamb without blemish,
the acceptable gift that gives you perfect praise.
At the Last Supper, seated with his apostles,
he left this memorial of his passion
to bring us its saving power until the end of time.
In this great sacrament you feed your people
and strengthen them in holiness,
so that throughout the world the human family
may be enlightened by one faith
and drawn together in one communion of love.
We come to this foretaste of your heavenly banquet
to be transformed by your grace
and restored in the image and likeness of the
    risen Christ.
Therefore earth unites with heaven
to sing a new song of praise;
we too join with angels and archangels
as they proclaim your glory without end:

Further material can be found in the Resources section of *New Patterns* under 'Holy Communion', and, of course, in the eucharistic sections of hymnbooks.

Dedication Festival

> Lord of the worlds above
> how pleasant and how fair
> the dwellings of thy love,
> thy earthly temples are!
> To thine abode
> my heart aspires,
> with warm desires
> to see my God.
>
> *Isaac Watts*

Isaac Watts' great metrical version of Psalm 84 picks up the great sense of joy and desire in coming together for worship. For many Anglicans this is bound up with affection for our parish churches, so many of them beautifully appointed and with a great sense of sacred space. This is the place where, week by week, God meets his people in grace, where God's mighty acts are celebrated, where prayer is offered and life consecrated. Of course, with the building go the people, our brothers and sisters in Christ, and strong bonds of memory, for the church is the place where the great events of life are celebrated, both in sorrow and in joy. An annual Dedication Festival provides an opportunity to give thanks for our churches, both buildings and people, as God's continuing faithfulness year by year is remembered and celebrated.

The *Common Worship* 'Rules to Order the Christian Year' (*Times and Seasons*, p. 27) state:

> The Dedication Festival of a church is the anniversary of the date of its dedication or consecration. This is kept either as a Festival or as a Principal Feast.
>
> When the date of dedication is unknown, the Dedication Festival may be observed on the first Sunday in October, or on the Last Sunday after Trinity, or on a suitable date chosen locally.

So there is a wide variety of choice. Of course, where the date is known, the instinct will be to keep it on or near that date (the Rules allow it to be transferred to the nearest Sunday when it is kept as a Principal Feast – but see the exceptions on page 27!). For some parishes, the first Sunday in October will be too close to Harvest Thanksgiving; for others, the Last Sunday after Trinity, while providing a festal end to the long 'after Trinity' period, will suffer as it tends to fall at school half-term. Excellent lectionary material can be found in the *Main Volume* (p. 587).

It should be noted that 'Dedication Festival' is something different from 'Patronal Festival'. 'Dedication Festival' relates to when a church was dedicated or consecrated, and so looks back to the establishment of a church building in that locality, whether ancient or modern. 'Patronal Festival' is the feast of title of a particular church (All Saints', St Mary's, St Peter's, Holy Cross, etc.), and so is related to the calendar, the day on which a saint or event in the Gospel story is commemorated. Here, *Common Worship: Festivals* comes into its own.

Times and Seasons resources

Much of the material in this section is drawn from *Enriching*:

- A1, Invitation to Confession
- B1, Kyrie Confession
- H1, Intercession
- J1, Introduction to the Peace
- L1, L2, Prefaces, from *ASB*
- P1, P2, Blessings (P2 has been re-ordered)
- R1, Acclamation.

There are three distinctive aspects of the *Times and Seasons* material. The first is the Prayer at the Preparation of the Table, drawing on Psalm 116.10, 11:

> Lord, teach us how to repay you for your goodness
>   towards us.
> We will lift up the cup of salvation
> and call upon your name.

The second is the Extended Preface, an enlarged version of a shorter preface from *Enriching*:

It is indeed right, our duty and our joy,
always and everywhere to give you thanks,
almighty and eternal Father,
enthroned upon the praises of your people.
We thank you for this house of prayer,
in which you bless your family
as we come to you in pilgrimage.
Here you reveal your presence in sacramental signs,
and make us one with you through the unseen bond of grace.
Here you build your temple of living stones,
and bring the Church to its full stature
as the body of Christ throughout the world,
to reach its perfection at last
in the heavenly city of Jerusalem,
which is the vision of your peace.
Therefore, in union with the heavenly Jerusalem,
with angels in joyful assembly,
with all whose names are written in heaven,
and with the spirits of the righteous made perfect,
we lift up our voices to join in the triumphal song of praise:

The third is An Alternative Dismissal, incorporating an Acclamation (R1, above), a dismissal Gospel (John 4.23, 24), an extended blessing (P2, above) and dismissal:

Like living stones, precious in his sight,
go in peace to proclaim the mighty acts of God.
Thanks be to God.

Bible Sunday

Help us, O Lord, to learn
the truths thy word imparts:
to study that thy laws may be
inscribed upon our hearts.
William Watkins Reid Jr

Bible Sunday, as such, has never appeared in any official Church of England calendar. The reason for this is that Bible Sunday was popularized by the various Bible societies and designated for Advent 2 because the Prayer Book collect relates to the Scriptures:

> Blessed Lord,
> who hast caused all holy Scriptures to be written for our
>   learning:
> Grant that we may in such wise hear them,
> read, mark, learn, and inwardly digest them,
> that by patience and comfort of thy holy Word,
> we may embrace and ever hold fast
> the blessed hope of everlasting life,
> which thou hast given us in our Saviour
>   Jesus Christ.
> **Amen.**

When the calendar was revised for *Common Worship*, it was recognized that the season of Advent had its own integrity, and so the Prayer Book collect was re-appointed for the Last Sunday after Trinity. This had an additional benefit in that it relates to 'Reformation Sunday', widely observed in the Protestant Churches of the continent on the last Sunday in October, and to the commemoration of Martin Luther in the *Common Worship* Calendar on 31 October. This was thus an appropriate liturgical response to ecumenical initiatives such as the Porvoo Agreement between the British and Irish Anglican Churches and the Nordic and Baltic Lutheran Churches and the Meissen Agreement between the Church of England and the German Protestant Church. So, while Bible Sunday is not mentioned in the Calendar, the *Common Worship* Lectionary makes provision for 'The Last Sunday after Trinity if observed as Bible Sunday' (*Main Volume*, p. 575), where readings for the Principal Service, Second Service and Third Service are given. This recognizes that Bible Sunday is widely observed in the Church of England, not least because it has been an opportunity to pray for the various societies and initiatives that seek to encourage the translation, printing and distribution of Bibles as well as resources to aid understanding of God's word. The *Additional Collects* provision recognizes this link, though in a subtle way:

> Merciful God,
> teach us to be faithful in change and in uncertainty,
> that trusting in your word
> and obeying your will
> we may enter the unfailing joy of Jesus Christ our Lord.

However, it can be equally argued that *every* Sunday is 'Bible Sunday', and so the *Times and Seasons* provision, in an opening note, outlines the possibilities for the Last Sunday after Trinity but adds,

> However, the following material may be used on any suitable occasion when the focus is on the word of God as revealed in holy Scripture.

The various Bible societies usually publish annual resources for worship. Additional resources may also be found in *New Patterns for Worship*, under the heading 'Word', and in 'Thanksgiving for the Word' in *Common Worship: Daily Prayer* (pp. 304–5). In the latter, the prayer of thanksgiving is resonant:

> Blessed are you, Lord our God.
> How sweet are your words to the taste,
> sweeter than honey to the mouth.
> How precious are your commands for our life,
> more than the finest gold in our hands.
> How marvellous is your will for the world,
> unending is your love for the nations.
> Our voices shall sing of your promises
> and our lips declare your praise.
> Blessed be God, Father, Son and Holy Spirit.
> **Blessed be God for ever.**

Times and Seasons resources

Some of these are drawn from the 'Word' section of *Enriching*:

- A1, Invitation to Confession
- B1, Kyrie Confession, slightly adapted

- H1, Intercessions

- P1, Blessing

- R1, Acclamation

However, there are a number of newly written texts:

- B2 provides an alternative Kyrie Confession:

> Your word convicts us:
> all have sinned and fallen short of the glory of God.
> Lord, have mercy.
> **Lord, have mercy.**
>
> Your word commands us:
> repent and believe the good news.
> Christ, have mercy.
> **Christ, have mercy.**
>
> Your word assures us:
> Christ Jesus came into the world to save sinners.
> Lord, have mercy.
> **Lord, have mercy.**

- H2 is a comprehensive form of Intercession for various ministries concerned with the Scriptures; two of the petitions give a flavour of the scope of the prayer:

> We give you thanks for all who distribute the Scriptures,
> and pray that, through the written text,
> your people may be built up in faith and love.
>
> Lord, hear us.
> **Lord, graciously hear us.**
>
> We give thanks for all whose learning interprets the
>   Scriptures,
> and pray for biblical scholars and theologians,
> that more light and truth may break forth from your word.
>
> Lord, hear us.
> **Lord, graciously hear us.**

- J1 and J2 are new introductory words to the Peace, the first drawing on Colossians 3.15, 16:

> Let the word of Christ dwell in you richly.
> Let the peace of Christ rule in your hearts.

and the second, from the Lent seasonal provision, chosen because it makes reference to the great Pauline and Reformed emphasis on justification by faith:

> Since we are justified by faith,
> we have peace with God through our Lord Jesus Christ,
> who has given us access to his grace.

- K1, the Prayer at the Preparation of the Table, makes reference to the 'table of the word' and the 'table of the sacrament':

> Lord Jesus,
> you nourish us at the table of your word
> and the table of your sacrament;
> as we feed on you, the bread of life,
> may we daily grow into your likeness.

- M1, the Extended Preface, weaves a series of biblical references:

> It is indeed right and good,
> our duty and our joy,
> always and everywhere to give you thanks,
> holy Father, almighty and eternal God,
> through Jesus Christ our Lord.
> For he is your eternal and creative Word,
> through whom all things came into being;
> the Word made flesh who dwelt among us,
> full of grace and truth.
> He fulfils the Law and the Prophets,
> dying for our sins and rising again
> in accordance with the Scriptures.
> He stands among us in his risen power;
> opening to us his living word,
> and making himself known in the breaking of the bread.

> Therefore with angels and archangels,
> and with all the company of heaven,
> we proclaim your great and glorious name,
> for ever praising you and saying:

- Finally, seven short passages of Scripture complete the section; some of them could be used as introductions and as responses to biblical readings, e.g.,

Reader A reading from the prophet Amos:
All **Speak, Lord, for your servant is listening.**

Or, at the end of a reading:

Reader Blessed are those who hear the word of God and obey it.
All **Thanks be to God.**

Or, using a text from the Christingle Service (*Times and Seasons*, p. 99)

Reader God's word is a lantern to our feet:
All **and a light to our path.**

At St David's, a major reordering project included the provision of a new holy table and lectern. The vicar recalled a conviction of Archbishop Donald Coggan that Anglicanism is *bi-focal* in its means of grace, in that God in Christ comes to us both by the sacraments and by the word. In order to give expression to this truth, both holy table and lectern were made from the same type of wood; both had specially designed seasonal falls using complementary designs, and both had specially designed candle-stands on each side. The new furniture thus demonstrated that we are fed at the table of God's word and at the table of his sacrament; both had an equal dignity. At the Eucharist, the Book of Lectionary Readings was carried in procession to the lectern; at a Service of the Word, the entire Bible. The free-standing candle-stands at the lectern were a visual reminder that God's word is a lamp to our feet and a light to our path, and of the conviction that God has yet more light and truth to shine forth from his word.

7 Seasons and Festivals of the Agricultural Year

> For the fruits of all creation,
>   thanks be to God;
> for the gifts to every nation,
>   thanks be to God;
> for the ploughing, sowing, reaping,
>   silent growth while we are sleeping,
> future needs in earth's safe keeping,
>   thanks be to God.
>
> *Fred Pratt Green*

All things visible and invisible

The two central creeds in Anglican worship, the Apostles' and Nicene Creeds, both begin with strong statements about God as creator:

> I believe in God, the Father almighty,
> creator of heaven and earth.
>
> We believe in one God,
> the Father, the Almighty,
> maker of heaven and earth,
> of all that is,
> seen and unseen.

However, there has been a widespread conviction that creation has not been a strong focus in recent liturgical revision. For example, the lack of lectionary material on creation in the Revised Common Lectionary has long been noted. In some ways, this is not surprising, as the lectionary takes as its starting point the Gospel reading, and it is a simple fact that the Gospels do not include much material on specifically creation-related themes. Or at least, where there are references to the natural world in the Gospels, for example in the parables, the overriding theme is something broader, such as Jesus' teaching about the kingdom of God. It was for this reason that the Liturgical Commission departed from the RCL provision for the Second Sunday before Lent in order to incorporate creation-based lections and Collects for that day. Hence, the appointed Collects are:

Almighty God,
you have created the heavens and the earth
and made us in your own image:
teach us to discern your hand in all your works
and your likeness in all your children;
through Jesus Christ your Son our Lord . . .

Main Volume, p. 390

Almighty God,
give us reverence for all creation
and respect for every person,
that we may mirror your likeness
in Jesus Christ our Lord.   *Additional Collects*, p. 11

The Principal Service Lectionary, similarly, draws fully on creation themes:

Year A

Genesis 1.1-23	In the beginning when God created the heavens and the earth
Psalm 136.1-9, [10-22], 23-26	who by his wisdom made the heavens
Romans 8.18-25	the creation waits with eager longing for the revealing of the children of God
Matthew 6.25-34	do not worry about your life, what you will eat or what you will drink

Year B

Proverbs 8.1, 22-31	The Lord created me at the beginning of his work

Psalm 104.26-37	O Lord, how manifold are your works!
Colossians 1.15-20	for in him all things in heaven and earth were created
John 1.1-14	all things came into being through him

Year C

Genesis 2.4b-9, 15-25	In the day that the Lord God made the earth and the heavens
Psalm 63	You visit the earth and water it; you make it very plenteous
Revelation 4	You are worthy, our Lord and God . . . for you created all things
Luke 8.22-25	The storm on the lake

This annual opportunity should be used to the full, adorned by the rich resources of creation hymnody and song.

Festivals and observances

Almost all churches observe Harvest Thanksgiving in one form or another, and many keep Rogationtide. While there is much diversity in the forms of service used on such occasions, and many parishes have time-honoured local traditions, the general creation material is supplemented in *Times and Seasons* by resources specific to Harvest and Rogationtide, along with two further festivals, Plough Sunday and Lammas, both of which have deep historic roots and have been revived with profit by some rural communities. *Times and Seasons*, therefore, includes resource materials, rather than fully worked-out services, for these festivals of the agricultural year, both as a means of providing *common* materials commended by the House of Bishops, and of suggesting how these important observances might be developed. It is undeniable that the material has a slant towards semi-rural and rural communities. This is not to minimize the often very good adaptation of, for example, Harvest Thanksgiving to more urban settings, but to recognize that such localized celebrations are not so strongly part of the Church's corporate liturgical memory. Some communities, both urban and rural, will wish, because of their proximity to the countryside, to make explicit in their liturgical programmes the importance of these celebrations as a matter of mission and affirmation of the agricultural industries and communities.

Creation

In common with other sections of *Times and Seasons*, a full range of
supplementary material is provided for use at the Holy Communion or
A Service of the Word. This material may profitably be used on the
Second Sunday before Lent to complement the creation-based biblical
passages set for that day, or on any suitable occasion when creation-
related themes are to the fore. This may include, for example, Christian
Aid Week, One World Week or services focusing on environmental
concerns. The material is also suitable for use at Rogationtide, Harvest
and other agricultural festivals.

Invitation to Confession Two forms are provided, the first adapted
from *Enriching the Christian Year* and the second from *New Patterns*,
both drawing on Romans 8 imagery.

Kyrie Confessions Of the three forms here, the first is from *Enriching*
and the second and third are new texts. The second draws on Jesus'
teaching in Matthew 6:

Consider the birds of the air;
they do not sow or gather into barns,
yet our heavenly Father feeds them.
Lord, have mercy.
Lord, have mercy.

Consider the lilies of the field, how they grow;
they do not toil nor spin,
yet even Solomon in all his glory was not arrayed like
one of these.
Christ, have mercy.
Christ, have mercy.

How little faith we have.
Seek first the kingdom of God and his righteousness.
Lord, have mercy.
Lord, have mercy.

The third was written by the Revd Kenneth Carveley, Methodist
Observer on the Liturgical Commission.

Gospel Acclamation A newly written text, drawing on Hebrews 1.2.

Intercession A new text, using the six days of creation from Genesis 1. This form could profitably be led by more than one voice, for example:

Voice 1   God said, 'Let the waters be gathered together,
and let dry land appear.'

Voice 2   We thank you for the beauty of the earth,
for the diversity of land and sea,
for the resources of the earth.
Give us the will to cherish this planet
and to use its riches for the good and welfare of all.
God of life:
hear our prayer.

It would also lend itself to visual presentations, using images of creation. The final collect, 'Heavenly Father, you have filled the world with beauty . . .' is adapted from the *BCP* of the Episcopal Church (USA), p. 814.

Introduction to the Peace This draws on Isaiah 55.12.

Prayers at the Preparation of the Table Two prayers commend themselves from the *Main Volume*: the 'grain once scattered' prayer derived from the *Didache*, and the prayer cast in the form of a Jewish *berakah*, 'Blessed be God, by whose grace creation is renewed . . .'

Prefaces The first text is newly written, making explicit reference to the 'new creation' inaugurated by the resurrection, and alluding to Romans 8. The second is an ICEL text included in *Enriching*.

Extended Preface A newly composed text, expressing the creative and redemptive work of the Trinity.

Blessings and Ending The short blessing was included in *Enriching*, having been written by C. L. MacDonell; the extended blessing is a new text:

May God the Father,
who clothes the lilies of the field
and feeds the birds of the air,
provide us with all we need for life in its fullness.
Amen.

May God the Son,
who fed the five thousand and turned water into wine,
feed us with his life and transform us in his love.
Amen.

May God the Holy Spirit,
who hovered over the waters of creation
and formed the world from chaos,
form us in the likeness of Christ and renew the face of
  the earth.
Amen.

And the blessing . . .

The dismissal text skilfully combines an exhortation to good stewardship with growth in holiness:

Tend the earth, care for God's good creation,
and bring forth the fruits of righteousness.
Go in the peace of Christ.
Thanks be to God.

Acclamations The first text draws on an adaptation of a Jewish *berakah* prayer, first published by the Anglican Church of Canada and also appearing in *The Promise of His Glory* as a 'Light Prayer'; the second uses imagery from the epiphany to Job, with part of Job's response as the repeated refrain.

Short Passages of Scripture Four texts are provided for use as part of the introduction or Post Communion, or as a repeated refrain throughout a service.

During One World Week, St Peter's Church decided to hold a weekend creation festival. This was intended as a development of the traditional 'flower festival', so as well as many flower arrangements, there was a series of DVD presentations on ecology, the environment, global warming, as well as material celebrating the diversity and wonder of creation. As the parish included significant numbers of people of other faiths, there were materials on what other faiths taught about creation and human responsibility. There were special features on Fair Trade. Local schools and the Junior Church and uniformed organizations provided artistic displays.

On Sunday morning a special all-age service was held. It adopted the following structure, using texts from *Times and Seasons* and *New Patterns*.

Gathering
As the congregation arrived, songs were led by the music group.

Greeting   The Lord be with you
                  and also with you.

Sentence   God saw everything that he had made:
                  and indeed it was very good.
                  (*Times and Seasons*, p. 606, S1)

Introduction   *The minister said words of welcome and set this*
                  service in the context of the Creation Festival

Praise and Adoration

Acclamation   Text from *New Patterns*, p. 226, G26

Opening prayer   Text from *New Patterns*, p. 240, G63

Hymn of praise

Penitence and Lament

Invitation to confession   Text from *Times and Seasons*,
                            p. 599, A2

Instrumental music and screen images (lament)

Confession   Text from *Times and Seasons*, p. 600, B3
Absolution

The Word of God
Reading
Drama
Short talk

Prayers

Intercession   Text from *Times and Seasons*, pp. 601–2, H1,
                led by two voices with projected images

The Lord's Prayer

*Hymn, during which the congregation assembled in the
churchyard.*

Blessings

Blessing of the earth   Text from *Times and Seasons*,
                           p. 610 (Rogation), H1

Congregational blessing   Text from *Times and Seasons*,
                           p. 604, P2

Dismissal   Text from *Times and Seasons*,
                           p. 604, P3

New Patterns for Worship provides, as a special example, a eucharistic service entitled 'All Creation Worships' (see pp. 458–78). It sets out a text for the congregation, an outline and leaders' text, and a full text for leaders, and so provides an excellent model for liturgical formation and good practice.

Plough Sunday

Ecclesiastes 3 reminds us that there is 'a time to plant and a time to pluck up what is planted'. Through the advances of modern farming technology, such times are ever variable, with much ploughing taking place towards the end of the calendar year. However, as the Introduction states (p. 597), the observance since Victorian times of Plough Sunday on the First Sunday after the Epiphany, reviving a much older tradition of marking the end of the Christmas holiday (Plough Monday), witnesses to an instinct that at the start of the calendar year we ask for God's blessing on the work of the year ahead. The plough continues to be a powerful symbol of preparation and of the potential of the earth's fruitfulness and fertility to sustain us in life. Churches which wish to revive this ceremony are at liberty to choose a suitable date, in consultation with the local farming community. The blessing of the plough or ploughshare may be done, if space permits, in church or in the churchyard, on a farm, either indoors or, weather permitting, out of doors. As such, it may be incorporated into a fuller act of worship, according to the pattern of services in any one locality.

The *Times and Seasons* provision includes two forms of blessing, the Blessing of the Plough, with the traditional acclamation 'God speed the plough', and the blessing of seed. In the latter case, the blessing may be adapted to include different types of seed or tuber.

The table of readings draws on biblical passages related to ploughing, sowing and seedtime:

Genesis 1.9-13	Let the earth put forth vegetation: plants yielding seed, and fruit trees of every kind on earth that bear fruit with the seed in it.
Genesis 8.20–9.3	As long as earth endures, seedtime and harvest, cold and heat, summer and winter, day and night, shall not cease.
Isaiah 55.6-11	giving seed to the sower and bread to the eater . . .
Ecclesiasticus 38.25-34	How can he become wise who handles the plough . . .
Psalm 37.22-38	and when the wicked are uprooted, you shall see it.
1 Corinthians 9.6-14	whoever ploughs should plough in hope and whoever threshes should thresh in hope of a share in the crop.
Matthew 6.25-34	Look at the birds of the air; they neither sow nor reap . . .

These longer readings are complemented by the Short Passages of Scripture; the quotation from Hosea 10.12 is particularly apt:

Sow for yourselves righteousness;
reap steadfast love;
break up your fallow ground;
for it is time to seek the Lord,
that he may come and rain righteousness upon you.

The form of blessing and dismissal provided is identical to the 'Creation' section.

Rogationtide

The Rogation Days, in both the Prayer Book and *Common Worship* calendars, are the three weekdays preceding Ascension Day. *Common Worship: Main Volume* provides two collects, the first 'for those who work on the land and sea' and the second 'for those engaged in commerce and industry' (p. 104). This encompasses the two major Rogationtide themes: prayer that the fruits of the earth may be given in due season, and petition for human work and industry. While the rogation days may be observed in those churches with daily services, there is also a longstanding tradition of observing the preceding Sunday (The Fifth Sunday After Easter in the Prayer Book; The Sixth Sunday of Easter in *Common Worship*) as 'Rogation Sunday'. The Latin verb *rogare*, to ask, is linked with the heavenly intercession of the ascended Christ, anticipated on the Sunday before Ascension Day. This was underlined by the Prayer Book Gospel reading from John 16, with the words 'Whatsoever ye shall ask the Father in my Name, he will give it you.' The *Common Worship* Principal Service Gospel readings do not reflect this tradition; they appoint Luke 24.44-53 in Years A and C, and John 15.9-17 in Year B. However, this does not prevent other Rogationtide elements being incorporated into worship on this day, whether at the Principal Service or a second or third service, whether eucharistic or non-eucharistic. The Easter hymn, 'Alleluia! Alleluia, hearts to heaven and voices raise', employs agrarian imagery and so is particularly suitable.

Times and Seasons provides Rogationtide material for use with the Holy Communion or A Service of the Word. The Invitation to Confession and Kyrie Confession recognize that we exploit the earth and fail properly to steward and share its resources:

Let us ask God to have mercy on our tired land,
and to prosper the work of our soiled hands.
Let us ask God to forgive our delusion of self-sufficiency
so that we may praise him for his provision and goodness.

Lord, you give us this good earth,
yet we take your generous gifts for granted.
Lord, have mercy.
Lord, have mercy.

> Lord, you give us this good earth,
> but we squander its rich resources.
> Christ, have mercy.
> **Christ, have mercy.**
>
> Lord, you give us this good earth,
> but we fail to share your bounty with all of your children.
> Lord, have mercy.
> **Lord, have mercy.**

Two forms of intercession are provided. The first, drawing on the ancient Rogationtide tradition of blessing the fields, and recognizing that God is the one from whom 'all blessings flow', uses the bold petition 'Upon the rich earth send a blessing, O Lord', with subsequent petitions for human labour, the earth's produce, the seas and waters, and aid agencies. The second form is a Christian Aid text, also used in *New Patterns*. The introduction to the Peace, from Philippians 4.6,7, picks up the theme of 'asking'. The Extended Preface is a new text, on the themes of creation–new creation. The acclamation draws on the Rogationtide psalm *par excellence*, Psalm 67.

The Rogationtide Procession

This is the distinctive provision for Rogationtide. George Herbert, in *The Country Parson*, writes:

> The Country Parson is a Lover of old Customs, if they be good, and harmless; and the rather, because Country people are much addicted to them, so that to favour them therein is to win their hearts, and to oppose them therein is to deject them. If there be any ill in the custom, that may be severed from the good, he pares the apple, and gives them the clean to feed on. Particularly, he loves Procession [i.e. beating the bounds], and maintains it, because there are contained therein four manifest advantages. First, a blessing of God for the fruits of the field: Secondly, justice in the Preservation of bounds: Thirdly, Charity in loving walking, and neighbourly accompanying one another, with reconciling of differences at that time, if there be any: Fourthly, Mercy in relieving the poor by a liberal distribution of largesse, which at

that time is, or ought to be used. Wherefore he exacts of all to be
present at the perambulation . . .

A Priest to the Temple, chapter 25

Two banks of material are provided. The first is a series of inserts into
both the *BCP* Litany and the *Common Worship* Litany. The inserts are
adapted from *The Book of Occasional Services* of the Episcopal
Church (USA). The second is a newly composed litany in six sections
with an appended bank of readings. The material does not have to be
used in procession; it can simply be used, in whole or in part, as a form
of intercession.

Where a procession does take place, it may be undertaken within a
church building if space permits, or in the open air.

The procession can take many forms; the following examples illustrate
some possibilities. The first example shows how adaptation of the texts
can include different localities and contexts.

St Michael's is a residential parish on the edge of a large town.
The large houses and cottages of the original 'village' are still
clearly visible, but behind them, on each side of the main road,
are large post-war local authority estates, one of them adjoining
a large industrial estate. To the north of the parish there is a huge
and growing modern estate, part private and part for rent
through a housing association. However, beyond this, and still
within the parish boundaries, are a variety of farms as the
urban townscape gives way to countryside. St Michael's
congregation is part resident in the parish and part eclectic. The
PCC was concerned to develop its ministry to the community.
At a PCC meeting, one of the churchwardens asked how well
the people of the church actually knew their own parish. So it
was agreed that on Rogation Sunday afternoon, a series of
'beating the boundaries' walks should be held, focusing on
different areas. Each group of walkers was given a notepad, and
members were asked to discuss and write down what they
observed. At various points, prayers were said. The rector used
the Rogationtide Litany from *Times and Seasons* as a starting
point, but rewrote and adapted it for the various areas of the
parish.

- Sections I, V and VI were used on each of the walks.

- Sections II and III were used by the group walking the rural fringe.

- Section IV was used on two of the estate walks, which passed the local row of shops, and the supermarket.

For the group walking through the industrial state, this litany was written:

For the Red House Industrial Estate, and for all the businesses on it:
Hear us, good Lord.

For all who find their employment here, and for their homes and loved ones:
Hear us, good Lord.

For those businesses that are thriving, and for their continued development and health:
Hear us, good Lord.

For those businesses that are struggling, and for all who are anxious about their future:
Hear us, good Lord.

For the problems of vandalism, and for those who are tempted to commit crime:
Hear us, good Lord.

For wisdom about the management of heavy traffic and for its impact on the environment:
Hear us, good Lord.

For all who live on the adjoining Red House estate, and for the ministry of the Church in this community:
Hear us, good Lord.

For the group walking through the post-war Highfield estate, this litany was written:

For the Highfield estate and all who live in it, let us pray to the Lord.
Lord, have mercy.

For Highfield Primary School, and for its governors, teachers, support staff and children, let us pray to the Lord.
Lord, have mercy.

For the Highfield Youth Centre, for its youth leaders and community worker, and for all who use the Centre and its facilities, let us pray to the Lord.
Lord, have mercy.

For Highfield Comprehensive School, and for its governors, teachers, support staff and students, let us pray to the Lord.
Lord, have mercy.

For the Highfield Health Centre, and for doctors, nurses, community nurses, midwives and for all struggling with illness and incapacity, let us pray to the Lord.
Lord, have mercy.

For every home, for those who live in families and those who live alone; for all with special needs, and for any in distress, let us pray to the Lord.
Lord, have mercy.

For the ministry of the Church in this community, let us pray to the Lord.
Lord, have mercy.

When each group returned, the observations were shared and discussed over a shared tea; for some, and especially those who lived outside the parish, their experience was an eye-opener. The outcomes were written up and became a major resource for the church's development of its ministry to its community. The experience also gave fresh impetus to the church as a praying community.

St Andrew's Church, noting that Rogationtide usually fell in close proximity to Christian Aid week, always organized an annual Christian Aid sponsored walk on the Saturday before Rogation Sunday, using a variety of pleasant routes in the semi-rural vicinity of the parish. At strategic points on the walk, one of the Short Passages of Scripture (*Times and Seasons*, p. 618), one of the readings from the table (*Times and Seasons*, p. 618) and a section of the *Common Worship* Litany were used, supplemented by some of the prayers from the annual Christian Aid pack. It became a popular and creative part of the annual parish programme.

The university campus was on the edge of the small city. Always on the look out for creative ways of engaging students, the Chaplain devised a Rogation walk. It began with a short service in the chapel:

Greeting
Acclamation: *Times and Seasons* p. 613, based on Psalm 67.
Hymn: five verses of 'All creatures of our God and King'
Invitation to Confession and Kyrie Confession: *Times and Seasons*, p. 609, B1, B2
Collect: *Main Volume*, p. 104.
Readings: Psalm 104.25-37;
             Matthew 6.7-15 (*Times and Seasons*, p. 618).
Prayers: *Times and Seasons*, p. 611, H2
Hymn   'God of mercy, God of grace'

At the edge of the campus, the form of Intercession on *Times and Seasons*, p. 610, H1 was used.

For the walk, which included woodland, passing the University Agricultural Centre, walking along a stretch of river, and crossing farmland, the sections of the Litany (*Times and Seasons*, pp. 615–17) and Table A of the readings (*Times and Seasons*, p. 618) were used. The walk finished at the local village hostelry!

Lammastide

Reference to Lammas Day appears in the Prayer Book Calendar for 1 August, even though no liturgical provision is made for its observance. Prior to the Reformation, an annual 'Loaf-Mass' was celebrated on 1 August in thanksgiving for the first-fruits of the wheat harvest. A specially baked loaf was presented before God as part of the mass for that day.

The *Times and Seasons* material, conscious of the origins of this observance, sets it in the context of a celebration of the Holy Communion. Where a celebration on or near 1 August is impractical, the setting of a suitable date is left to local discretion. The introductory note states that the Lammas loaf, or probably part of it, may be used as the eucharistic bread or kept separate from it. Certainly, there should be no confusion about what bread is the consecrated bread of the Eucharist. For that reason, the Presentation of the Lammas loaf is made as part of the Gathering, or could precede a celebration of communion according to the Prayer Book rite.

The Lammas loaf

- The loaf should be large enough to be carried in procession as a vivid visual symbol.

- Preferably, it should be baked using local ingredients by a member of the local community.

- Symbols, made from the dough, may be used. These may include representations of wheat, a sickle, a basket, loaves and fishes, a chalice, a cross.

- Preferably, it should be presented by members of the local farming community, and those who have baked the bread.

- Where the Lammas loaf is not the eucharistic loaf, it should not be placed on the holy table, but it may be placed before the table or in a suitable place where it is visible to the congregation.

The Gathering rite has the following elements

- Greeting

- Introduction by the president
- procession of the Lammas loaf
- blessing of the Lammas loaf
- Prayers of penitence, including Kyrie Confession based on the Lord's Prayer
- (Gloria in Excelsis)
- Collect

Further resources are provided: two sets of Bible readings (the first on the offering of first-fruits, and the second on the Bread of Life), the 'Blessed are you' prayers for the Preparation of the Table and Post Communion, and texts for the Blessing and Dismissal. Where the Lammas loaf has not been used for communion, or where the Lammas celebration is non-eucharistic, the loaf may be broken and shared informally as a sign of fellowship, rather like the tradition of distributing blessed bread or *antidoron* in the Orthodox tradition.

In some places, the offering of first-fruits may take other forms; for example, the bringing of the first fleece in hill-farming communities. The *Times and Seasons* material can readily be adapted in such circumstances.

Harvest Thanksgiving

Of all the agricultural festivals, Harvest Thanksgiving is by far the most commonly celebrated, and forms a central place in the autumn programme for many churches and schools. Many communities, whether rural or urban, know instinctively how they wish to celebrate this festival; many traditions are time-honoured and expectations that these traditions will be observed are high. Perhaps the most common forms of service are:

- traditional Prayer Book Evensong, with Psalm 65 sung to Anglican chant
- a Harvest Parish Communion
- an All-Age Service, with presentation of Harvest gifts
- a Harvest 'Songs of Praise'

Many churches have more than one service, sometimes to cater for different constituencies. Moreover, many mission societies and aid agencies prepare creative and attractive worship resources for Harvest, drawing attention particularly to needs in the developing world. Some churches have departed from 'traditional' approaches to Harvest altogether, and have sought to give expression to other aspects of the provision of the necessities of life, perhaps celebrating local productivity or responding to local needs such as provision for homeless people.

Common Worship: Main Volume provides a number of resources for Harvest:

- Collect and Post Communion Prayer (contemporary p. 447, traditional p. 521)

- Confession, p. 126

- Lectionary, p. 588 (three-year cycle)

- Sentence of Scripture, Morning and Evening Prayer, *BCP*, p. 60

In the Rules to Order the Christian Year, it is stated that Harvest Thanksgiving may be celebrated on a Sunday and replace the provision for that day, provided it does not supersede a Principal Feast or Festival (p. 530, cf. p. 534). *New Patterns for Worship* includes an outline for a non-sacramental service suitable for all ages (see pp. 432–4), as well as suitable texts in the Resource Sections.

In the light of the above, the approach in *Times and Seasons* is to provide further resources.

The penitential texts include a newly written Invitation to Confession and three Kyrie Confessions, the first two written by the Liturgical Commission and the third from *New Patterns*, and the form of responsorial confession from *Main Volume*, p. 126.

A distinctive addition to the usual bank of resources is a section specifically on Thanksgiving. This underlines the *Common Worship* title Harvest *Thanksgiving* rather than Harvest *Festival*. This responsorial thanksgiving was written by Kenneth Carveley, who also wrote the second form of intercession (H2, p. 628). The first form of intercession is adapted from *Enriching the Christian Year*.

Another distinctive addition to the Harvest bank of resources is 'The Bringing Forward of the Symbols of the Harvest'. This is adapted from a form originally prepared by the Yorkshire Agricultural Society and suggested by the Ven. Clive Mansell. It gives shape to a creative and comprehensive procession of Harvest gifts, and the Commission was pleased to include a text mentioning mangolds! The list of items for procession may, of course, be adapted according to the nature of the produce grown in a particular locality. The text assumes a eucharistic context, but this too can be easily adapted for non-eucharistic occasions. The familiar doxology at the end may be said or sung, and the refrain 'Thanks be to God' may be replaced by a suitable sung chant or 'alleluia'.

The Prayers at the Preparation of the Table are the familiar and ancient Jewish blessing prayers of bread and wine, also used at the Eucharist of Maundy Thursday. The short preface is an ICEL prayer. The two forms of blessing are from the Church in Wales.

Prayer in Times of Agricultural Crisis

The Book of Common Prayer includes prayers for rain, for fair weather, and in time of dearth and famine. Two prayers are provided in *Times and Seasons*: the first is an adaptable prayer for use 'in Times of Crisis', and the second a prayer 'for Favourable Weather in Time of Need', from the *Book of Common Prayer* of the Episcopal Church (USA). The intention is that such prayers may be made on a daily or regular basis in times of crisis such as the foot and mouth outbreak of 2001 or the severe flooding of 2007.

Embertide

Ember Days, as the note on page 636 of *Times and Seasons* sets out, are observed in the week before an ordination, or as designated days of prayer 'for those who serve the Church in its various ministries, both ordained and lay, and for vocations'. The traditional Ember Days are the Wednesdays, Fridays and Saturdays before

- the Third Sunday in Advent, where the Collect (*BCP* and *CW*) prays for the 'ministers and stewards of your mysteries'

- the Second Sunday of Lent

- the Sunday nearest 29 June (Petertide, St Peter and St Paul)

- the Sunday nearest 29 September (Michaelmas).

In *Times and Seasons*, the Embertide provision follows the Agricultural Year, and this is appropriate as the origins of the Ember Days probably lie in agricultural festivals around the quarter days, marking the four seasons. This is reflected in the Short Passages of Scripture (p. 642) where three of the four use agricultural imagery:

> Look around you,
> and see how the fields are ripe for harvesting.   *John 4.35*
>
> You did not choose me but I chose you.
> And I appointed you to go and bear fruit, fruit that
>   will last.   *John 15.16*
>
> The harvest is plentiful but the labourers are few;
> therefore, ask the Lord of the harvest
> to send out labourers into his harvest.
>   *Matthew 9.37, 38*

The bank of resources draws on the 'Ministry' section in *Enriching*:

- A1, Invitation to Confession

- H1, Intercession

- J1 (adapted) and J2, Introductions to the Peace

- L2, preface, drawn from *ASB*

- R1, Acclamation

Among the new texts,

- A2, Invitation to Confession, draws on 1 Peter 2.9

- B1, Kyrie Confession adapts the three short passages of Scripture quoted above

- K1, the Prayer at the Preparation of the Table, is suitable for use on a variety of occasions:

> Heavenly Father,
> as we set before you these gifts of bread and wine,
> bless also the gifts of our hearts and minds
> as we offer our lives in your service;
> for Jesus Christ's sake.

- M1, Extended Preface, skilfully combines material from the Extended Prefaces for the Ordination of Deacons and the Ordination of Priests from *Common Worship: Ordination Services*.

- P1, Blessing, is a creative text, relating ministry to the work of the Spirit:

> May the boldness of the Spirit transform you,
> may the gentleness of the Spirit lead you,
> may the gifts of the Spirit equip you
> to serve and worship God;
> and the blessing . . .

Other material may be adapted from *Common Worship: Ordination Services* and the 'Church and Mission' resource section of *New Patterns*. *New Patterns* also includes some 'words for dedication' responsories, suitable for the dedication of church officers, PCC members, and stewardship or mission visitors.

Conclusion

The first of these books on using *Times and Seasons* began by talking about a banquet, but ended with a warning about the danger of enrichment leading to indigestion! The concept of 'less is more' is one that can usefully be applied to the rich spread of resources in *Times and Seasons*. Another *caveat* is that the fully worked orders of service in *Times and Seasons* are examples of how liturgies *may* be celebrated rather than how they *must* be celebrated. Once again, the need to make 'wise and discriminating choices' is clear.

This being said, many churches continue to find their worship to be enriched by the use of seasonal material. When thoughtful and well-chosen text, appropriate music and symbolism, and good and varied liturgical leadership combine, the Christian Year becomes dynamic and exciting: a vehicle for praise and a tool for teaching and mission.

Times and Seasons has been published at a time when, increasingly, Anglicans are learning to harness and develop the creativity found in many Christian people. Developments in shared ministry mean that there are now opportunities for many lay people to contribute to the ordering of worship – it is no longer a merely clerical preserve, dependent upon the energy and creativity (or lack of it) of the incumbent.

The full potential of *Times and Seasons* will be truly discovered only if Christian communities think and plan collaboratively, asking together '*how* we shall celebrate the great truths of incarnation and redemption, which stand at the heart of the gospel.' This requires good planning, good teaching, and all the resources of Bible and tradition. It means harnessing all the gifts of word and music, symbol and ceremonial, imagination and flair. It demands that we give as much attention to enactment as to text, and that the important theological truths embedded in the liturgy are explored and applied to active

Christian discipleship. Then, indeed, the banquet of worship leads not to indigestion but to transformation, the making of a people truly for God's own possession, so that his salvation might reach to the ends of the earth.

Index of subjects

absolutions
  Ash Wednesday 32
  Easter 106
Acclamations
  Ascension to Pentecost 120
  Creation 151
  Easter 84, 85, 88, 92, 93, 95, 98, 99, 103, 116
  Easter season 110
  Lent 22, 27
  Passiontide 55
  Rogationtide 156
  Trinity Sunday 132
  see also Gospel Acclamations
Act of Penitence, Easter 105–7
Additional Collects 28, 37, 45, 54–5, 141–2, 147
Adkins, Donna 130
agape 69–71
agriculture
  agricultural year 146–66
  Prayer in times of crisis 164
Alexander, C. F. 130
all-age services
  Ascension Day 117–18
  and Creation 152
  Easter 88, 96
  Good Friday 72
  Mothering Sunday 37
  Palm Sunday 61
  Pentecost 127
  Stations of the Resurrection 112
Alleluia
  at Easter 99, 103
  not used in Lent 18, 21, 29
altar of repose 68
Alternative Service Book 2, 22, 48, 104, 108–9, 119, 131, 136, 165
Ambrose of Milan 5
Annunciation 43
anointing, at Pentecost 123–5
anthems, Good Friday 75
Ascension Day 10, 115–18
  blessings 117
  Dismissal 116–17

  Gathering 115–16
  Reading 115–16
Ascension to Pentecost 10–11
  Blessings 120
  Extended Preface 120
  Intercession 119
  Invitation to Confession 119
  Kyrie Confessions 119
  Peace, introductions to 119
  Preparation of the Table 119
  seasonal material 118–21
Ash Wednesday 6–7, 21, 27–33
  Blessings 22
  Collects 28
  Dismissal 33
  Gathering 28
  Gospel 34
  imposition of ashes 29
  Introduction 6
  Liturgy of Penitence 28, 29–32
  Liturgy of the Sacrament 32–3
  Liturgy of the Word 28–9
  Prayer after Communion 32
  Prefaces 7, 32
  Preparation of the Table 32
  Readings 28
  see also Shrove Tuesday
Augustine of Hippo 4–5
Aulén, Gustaf 9
austerity, Lenten 18, 32, 36, 59, 65, 73

Bairstow, Edward 68
banners
  at Ascension Day 116
  at Easter 99
baptism
  and Easter Liturgy 82, 85
  in Easter Vigil 5, 19, 20, 85, 93
  and Lent 17, 18–20, 26, 32
  and Paschal Candle 129
  at Pentecost 121
  and Trinity Sunday 130
  water 98–9
beating the bounds 156, 157–9
Beatitudes 24, 30

Index of biblical references